TRUST
— AT A —
DISTANCE
6 Strategies for Managing
in Remote Workspaces

DAVID HORSAGER
AND **PEGGY KENDALL**

Berrett–Koehler Publishers, Inc.

Berrett-Koehler Publishers, Inc.
1333 Broadway, Suite P100
Oakland, CA 94612-1921
Tel: (510) 817-2277
Fax: (510) 817-2278
bkconnection.com

ORDERING INFORMATION

Quantity sales. Special discounts are available on quantity purchases by corporations, associations, and others. For details, please go to bkconnection.com to see our bulk discounts or contact bookorders@bkpub.com for more information.

Individual sales. Berrett-Koehler publications are available through most bookstores. They can also be ordered directly from Berrett-Koehler: Tel: (800) 929-2929; Fax: (802) 864-7626; bkconnection.com.

Orders for college textbook/course adoption use. Please contact Berrett-Koehler: Tel: (800) 929-2929; Fax: (802) 864-7626.

Distributed to the US trade and internationally by Penguin Random House Publisher Services.

The authorized representative in the EU for product safety and compliance is EU Compliance Partner, Pärnu mnt. 139b-14, 11317 Tallinn, Estonia, www.eucompliancepartner.com, +372 5368 65 02.

Berrett-Koehler and the BK logo are registered trademarks of Berrett-Koehler Publishers, Inc.

Printed in the United States of America

Berrett-Koehler books are printed on long-lasting acid-free paper. When it is available, we choose paper that has been manufactured by environmentally responsible processes. These may include using trees grown in sustainable forests, incorporating recycled paper, minimizing chlorine in bleaching, or recycling the energy produced at the paper mill.

Library of Congress Cataloging-in-Publication Data
Names: Horsager, David author | Kendall, Peggy author
Title: Trust at a distance : 6 strategies for managing in remote workspaces / David Horsager, Peggy Kendall.
Description: First edition. | Oakland, CA : Berrett-Koehler Publishers, Inc, [2026] | Includes bibliographical references and index.
Identifiers: LCCN 2025022375 (print) | LCCN 2025022376 (ebook) | ISBN 9798890571083 hardcover | ISBN 9798890571090 pdf | ISBN 9798890571106 epub
Subjects: LCSH: Telecommuting | Flexible work arrangements | Industrial management | Leadership | Trust
Classification: LCC HD2336.3 .H68 2026 (print) | LCC HD2336.3 (ebook)
LC record available at https://lccn.loc.gov/2025022375
LC ebook record available at https://lccn.loc.gov/2025022376

First Edition
33 32 31 30 29 28 27 26 25   10 9 8 7 6 5 4 3 2 1

Book production: Happenstance Type-O-Rama
Cover design: Ashley Ingram

Contents

INTRODUCTION

It happened again.

We were in the middle of a virtual team workshop, staring at ten silent faces in ten tiny squares in front of ten fake backgrounds, every one of the participants feeling just fine saying absolutely nothing. This leadership team—highly experienced, fully remote, and responsible for guiding a global organization—was struggling to build a cohesive culture. The problem wasn't a lack of intelligence or drive; it was a lack of trust. You could see it in their faces—or rather, you couldn't see *anything* in their faces. They simply sat awkwardly in that distant digital space, each person seemingly waiting for someone else to say something honest, or say anything at all.

It made sense.

If we had been in the same room—breathing the same air, sharing the same space—it would have been different. There would have been a natural rhythm, subtle nods of agreement, quiet asides, and a collective momentum that would have built as the conversation progressed. But here we were, divided by screens and fragmented by distance, asking what trust meant to them and, in return, getting nothing but silence.

The Reality of Remote Work

Unfortunately, this situation isn't unique. Leaders across industries are facing the same challenge: *How do you build trust when you are never really WITH your people?*

Trust is foundational to every high-performing team. It accelerates productivity, increases engagement, and strengthens loyalty. Yet, in the shift to remote and hybrid work, many of the organic ways trust develops—casual conversations in the hallway, spontaneous check-ins, exchanges of nonverbal cues—have disappeared. The usual ways of leading no longer work like they once did.

The good news? Remote work isn't a trust killer. In fact, with the right strategies, trust can be built even *more* intentionally in virtual spaces than in traditional offices.

But here's the challenge: Trust at a distance is different.

Communicating through screens and texts fundamentally changes how we work, how we think, how we build relationships, and how we build trust. It requires different strategies because threats to trust—miscommunication, isolation, lack of visibility—are embedded in every digital interaction. Leaders can't assume that replicating an in-person office in a virtual setting will be enough.

That's why this book exists.

The Tensions You're Facing Right Now

If you're leading in a remote or hybrid environment, you already understand the unique tensions that make building and sustaining trust so difficult. Here are just a few:

- Lifeless virtual meetings where no one speaks up
- Cryptic emails that leave you wondering what's really going on
- Lack of spontaneity, where you can't just walk into someone's office to ask a simple question
- Employees who feel invisible, disconnected, isolated, or unsure of their role
- Managers who struggle to trust their teams because they can't physically see them working
- A culture that feels fragmented and inconsequential

These aren't small frustrations—they are symptoms of a workplace in transition.

Who We Are and Why We Wrote This Book

Meet **David**—global trust expert, bestselling author, and advisor to Fortune 500 CEOs and government leaders. He has spent his career studying the impact of trust on performance and advising organizations on how to implement high-trust leadership strategies. He holds a D.Litt. from Indiana Wesleyan University and has worked with a wide cross-section of industries and organizations.

Meet **Peggy**—a Ph.D. researcher and professor of communication studies. Ever since MySpace logged its way onto the scene in 2003, she has been researching how technology impacts human connection, workplace relationships, and leadership effectiveness.

When we (David and Peggy) bumped into each other at a local coffee shop one sunny afternoon, we quickly discovered we were both working with leaders facing the same kinds of problems. As we shared stories, we realized something powerful: Remote and hybrid work environments aren't just challenges to overcome—they're opportunities to **rethink** how culture is supported and trust is built.

The Unexpected Upside of Remote Work

Through our work, we have witnessed many surprising benefits when people move their desks from the office to their homes. We have seen employees who are working out of the line of sight of their supervisors suddenly feel more trusted and become even more motivated to innovate and work hard. We have seen teams where trust propels members to take more chances, feel more truly included, and become more authentically engaged than when they met face to face every day. And we have seen organizations where leaders intentionally create alignment, allowing geographically dispersed employees to work toward a unified mission with even more clarity and purpose than ever before.

We have worked with excited executives who have **cracked the code** on remote leadership, fostering high-trust, high-performance cultures without relying on outdated in-office habits. Their success is what inspired this book.

What You'll Learn

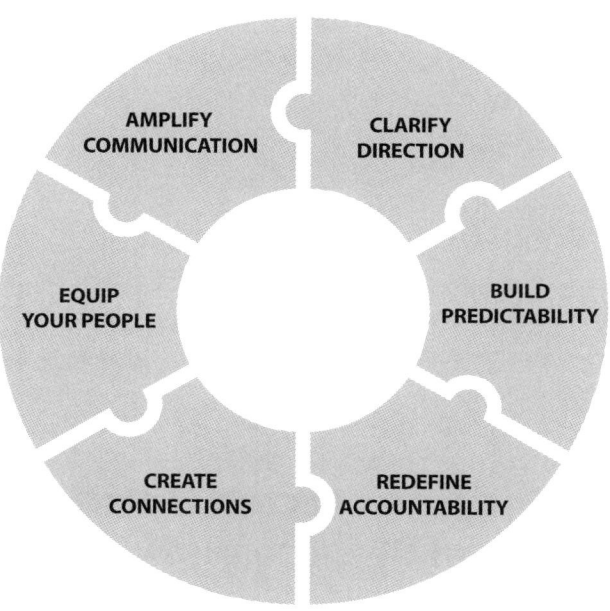

Through our combined fifty-five years of experience, we've designed six key strategies for building trust in remote and hybrid workplaces:

Strategy 1: Amplify Communication—Don't assume people will get it if you don't say it. Overcommunicate, provide clear information, and be careful about the stories you tell yourself.

Strategy 2: Clarify Direction—Keep everyone headed toward the same goal. Without physical proximity, vision will blur. Regularly reinforce the organization's Mission, Values, and Priorities.

Strategy 3: Build Predictability—Increase feelings of safety with reliable points of contact. In the absence of informal interactions, predictable, structured check-ins reduce the uncertainty that naturally arises in distant spaces.

Strategy 4: Redefine Accountability—Ditch the time clock and embrace accountable autonomy. Build motivation by focusing on results, not time spent sitting at a desk.

Strategy 5: Create Connections—Reduce the distance by strengthening belongingness. Intentional effort to foster relationships and team culture prevents isolation.

Strategy 6: Equip Your People—Train, supply, and update. Don't let remoteness impact excellence. Be sure to provide the right tools and development opportunities for dispersed employees to thrive.

Trust can be built at a distance! It takes a few strategic adjustments, lots of intentionality, and a clear commitment to make it work.

The successful
workplace isn't
defined by walls,
it's defined by trust.

IT'S A WHOLE NEW DAY
Same job, more opportunities.

No matter how history ultimately judges the great work-from-home movement of the 21st century, one thing is certain: *There's no going back.* The traditional office, once viewed as an immovable pillar of business, has been fundamentally reshaped by technology, shifting priorities, and the indisputable advantages of a dispersed workforce. And while we can pine for the way work used to be, we simply can't ignore the opportunities created by offices that are no longer constrained by the physical walls of a building.

Why Remote? The Clear Benefits of a Dispersed Workforce

For those still questioning whether remote work is a good long-term strategy, consider the benefits:

- **A larger talent pool:** Companies can now hire the best talent *from anywhere.* No longer limited by geography, organizations can access a diverse range of skills, perspectives, and experiences.[1]

- **Increased productivity:** According to a Harvard Business School study, remote workers spend an average of *48.5 more minutes per day* engaged in work-related activities than their in-office peers.[2] In a separate GitLab study, remote employees cited *higher efficiency, fewer distractions, and reduced office politics* as major remote benefits for the organization.[3]

- **Saved time:** A 2023 study from the National Bureau of Economic Research found that remote workers save approximately *72 minutes per day* in commute and prep time. That's over *6 hours a week*—time that can be spent on things more important than a daily commute.[4]

- **A greener footprint:** A fully remote worker can reduce their greenhouse gas emissions by up to 54 percent. Less travel means fewer cars on the road, lower energy consumption, and a more sustainable future.[5]

- **Financial savings:** Financial analyses have found that start-ups can save up to $10,600 per employee per year by reducing expenses related to office rent, utilities, and perks like snacks and coffee.[6]

- **Better housing fit:** Remote work has freed employees from the necessity of living close to an office. A survey by Apartment List found that 36 percent of fully remote workers planned to move within the next year, often choosing more affordable cities or locations closer to family.[7]

- **Increased inclusion and diversity:** Remote work removes many of the barriers that have traditionally kept marginalized groups from thriving in office settings. It minimizes the social pressure of being the "only" in a room, reduces unconscious biases that come with in-person interactions, and opens career opportunities for those who may not previously have had access.[8]

- **Greater accessibility:** For people with disabilities, remote work eliminates many of the challenges of commuting and working in physical spaces that aren't designed with accessibility in mind. It allows them to contribute at the highest levels without unnecessary obstacles.[9]

- **Stronger documentation and transparency:** Unlike traditional workplaces where ideas are often lost in conversation, digital collaboration tools automatically create records of decisions, feedback, and project updates.[10]

- **Leveling the playing field:** The remote workplace creates a more balanced space for different personality types. Introverts can get a word into digital discussions without the stress of trying to force their way into extrovert-dominated conversations.[11]

The shift to remote work isn't about avoiding the office—it's about **optimizing the way we work** and leveraging technology to build stronger, more flexible organizations.

Why Trust Matters

While the benefits of remote work are clear, the transition hasn't been without struggle. Whether through the increasingly hostile debate about whether people working from home are really "working" or contentious return-to-office (RTO) mandates that result in strikes, lawsuits, employee resignations, and damaged relationships, these virtual work solutions have placed unique stresses on how trust is built—and lost. With so much extra distance, so much unseen and unsupervised work, and so many stereotypes and assumptions exchanged between leaders and employees, it has become increasingly clear that **trust is more important than ever.**

But why is *trust* the answer to the remote dilemma? We define trust as **the confident belief an individual has in a person, product, or organization**. When trust exists, teams move faster, collaborate more effectively, and innovate with confidence. Research shows that trusted leaders have a measurable competitive advantage. Here are just a few of the benefits:

- **Greater retention:** Research from MIT suggests that trusting employees are 50 percent less likely to look for another job compared to those in low-trust environments.[12] A recent Trust Edge Leadership Institute report found that, next to compensation, *working for a trusted leader is the number-one reason employees stay with their company.*[13]

- **Higher performance and energy:** Paul Zak, director of the Center for Neuroeconomic Studies, found that employees who trust their leaders report being:

  50 percent more productive

  106 percent more energized at work

  74 percent less stressed

  40 percent less likely to experience burnout[14]

- **Stronger commitment:** Employees in high-trust workplaces don't just show up for a paycheck—they're *emotionally invested* in the company's mission. A 2018 HR.com study found that trust in leadership is the top driver of employee engagement, ranking higher than even company culture and career growth opportunities.[15]

- **Better communication and innovation:** Teams with high trust levels are more willing to share ideas, voice concerns, and take creative risks. Studies consistently show trusted team members feel empowered to challenge assumptions, solve problems collaboratively, and think beyond what's "safe" or expected.[16]

Regardless of where our workplaces are located, it is a culture of trust that motivates employees, binds them together, and propels them to achieve goals they could never accomplish on their own. When we combine the **opportunities of remote work** with the **positive outcomes of trust**, it is quite possible that a trust-filled virtual workplace can create even **more** meaningful relationships and a **deeper** sense of commitment than we have ever experienced in the traditional in-person office.

Understanding the New Trust Challenges

A key to understanding how trust operates in the remote workplace is to acknowledge the fundamental ways virtual workplaces differ from traditional offices.

First is the challenge of information. In remote work, employees lack everyday nonverbal cues that provide context and emotional depth. According to early communication scholars, only 7 percent of our communication is conveyed through words.[17] That means 93 percent of what we are trying to communicate is conveyed nonverbally, using cues like how we sit, how close we stand, how we use eye contact, and even how we change our voice.[18] These are exactly the kinds of cues that begin to disappear as we increasingly rely on digital connections to get our message across. The result is less information to work with and more opportunity for misunderstanding.

Second is the challenge of relationships. Without spontaneous in-person interactions, team connections weaken and colleagues become increasingly isolated. We can't underestimate the value of workplace relationships. Coworkers not only provide important sources of support and a feeling of belongingness but also keep us accountable and help define who we are and how we are doing. As distance reduces the natural flow of relational communication, it is all too easy for employees to become disconnected and less committed to the team and the work of the organization.

The Stories We Tell Ourselves

When we operate with less information and fewer relationships, something happens. We start to fill in what is missing with our own assumptions. We draw on past experience, add in little bits of information we've picked up here and there, and suddenly have fully developed plotlines that help explain *what* people are thinking and *why* they are choosing to do the things they do. Pretty soon, the stories we tell ourselves about our colleagues loom larger than reality itself. This is one of the most vexing challenges with virtual communication—we get used to operating with less information and rarely attempt to discern what we *actually* know from what we *assume* we know.

To succeed in a virtual workplace, we need new trust-building strategies that actively reduce these deficits in information and relationships and reduce the need for creative storytelling.

Clarifying Your Attitude toward Remote Work

Before we dive into strategies, let's take a moment for a little honest reflection.

No matter your role—CEO, manager, team lead, or frontline employee—your **mindset** about remote work directly impacts how you lead and collaborate in this environment. If you view it as a temporary inconvenience, a diluted version of "real" work, or just something that you need to tolerate, your leadership, communication, and expectations will reflect that skepticism.

On the other hand, if you embrace the new way of working as legitimate and powerful, you'll unlock higher levels of engagement, efficiency, and trust within your team.

We have to be honest—this shift hasn't been easy. And that's why, before we examine how to build trust in a remote workplace, we first need to ask: *What's YOUR attitude toward remote work?* The self-assessment on the next page is designed to help you start thinking through where you stand right now.

Final Thought: Your Mindset Matters

Trust isn't just about policies, check-ins, or fancy collaboration tools—it starts with *how you see your people.*

Even in our small team, we have experienced some major shifts. For example, Peggy has always been a lover of remote possibilities, enjoying the freedom to work with people from across the country in ways that fit the lifestyle of an adventure-seeking world traveler.

David, however, has been on a more roundabout remote journey. At the start, he believed in-person environments were far superior for fostering collaboration, a cohesive culture, and high performance. But in the process of putting this book together, as he did research, had remote conversations, and hired his first fully remote employee, trust, communication, and accountability flourished. He witnessed firsthand benefits such as access to top-tier talent at a lower cost, greater flexibility, and the creation of a high-performing team without geographic limits. Through the process of seeking to better understand the constraints and possibilities of remote work, we have both come to appreciate and embrace the good things that happen when trust is built in remote and hybrid workspaces.

Mindset matters! If you assume employees won't be productive unless they're in sight, you'll build systems of control that lead to frustration and disengagement. If you assume the remote work model is inherently weak, you'll resist making the necessary adjustments to make it strong.

But if you choose to believe that trust, culture, and performance can thrive at a distance—which *they absolutely can*—you'll be ready to lead with confidence and build an organization where people feel **empowered, supported, and trusted**. And that's where the real transformation begins.

Trusted Leader Advice

Bobby Herrera, president of the Populus Group, has found that the number-one key to leading successful remote workplaces is to publicly commit. He says, "There are plenty of leaders out there who are experiencing a sort of 'psychological tug of war,' feeling like the remote work approach might not be worth it. I finally said to my leadership team, 'Look, I loved *those days* as much as you did. But we're in a new chapter now, and you know, the chapters we write tomorrow are going to be better written together. So, let's accept it, and let's get into it!'"[19]

Self-Assessment: Where Do I Stand?

Take a few minutes to answer the following questions. Be honest. Your responses will help you identify where you may need to shift your mindset, clarify concerns, or have deeper conversations with your team.

1. **I believe it's possible to build a strong workplace culture in a remote environment.**

   1 = No way—I think company culture dies outside the office.

   5 = Yes! Remote culture can be as strong as, if not stronger than, in-person.

   1   2   3   4   5

2. **What are my biggest concerns about remote work?**

3. **I trust my remote employees to work hard and be productive.**

   1 = I can't trust them if I can't see them.

   5 = I believe remote work actually enhances productivity.

   1   2   3   4   5

4. **What, specifically, causes me the most distrust in remote work?**

5. **I believe most of my employees enjoy working remotely.**

   1 = No, I think they hate it; most miss those good old office days.

   5 = Yes, most love it and thrive in this environment!

   1   2   3   4   5

6. Why do I think my employees feel the way they do about remote work?

7. What benefits does a fully remote or hybrid model bring to my company? *(Think beyond cost savings.)*

8. What would the ideal remote or hybrid workplace look like for my organization?

Applying Your Results

Now that you've completed the self-assessment, take a step back and look at your responses:

Did you identify gaps that might exist between your thinking and that of your employees?

If so, it's time for deeper conversations. Talk to your team. Listen to their experiences. You may be surprised by what they find most valuable—and what frustrates them the most.

Did you recognize any attitudes that could be limiting trust?

If you scored low on trust, be honest about why. Is it because of a lack of structure? A fear of losing control? What steps could you take to increase clarity, accountability, and connection without resorting to micromanagement?

Did you uncover new challenges or advantages to remote work that you hadn't considered?

Use this insight to collaborate with your leadership team and employees to optimize your remote or hybrid strategy. Whether you're struggling with alignment, engagement, or efficiency, there are solutions. *(Don't worry—we've packed this book with plenty of ideas to get you started.)*

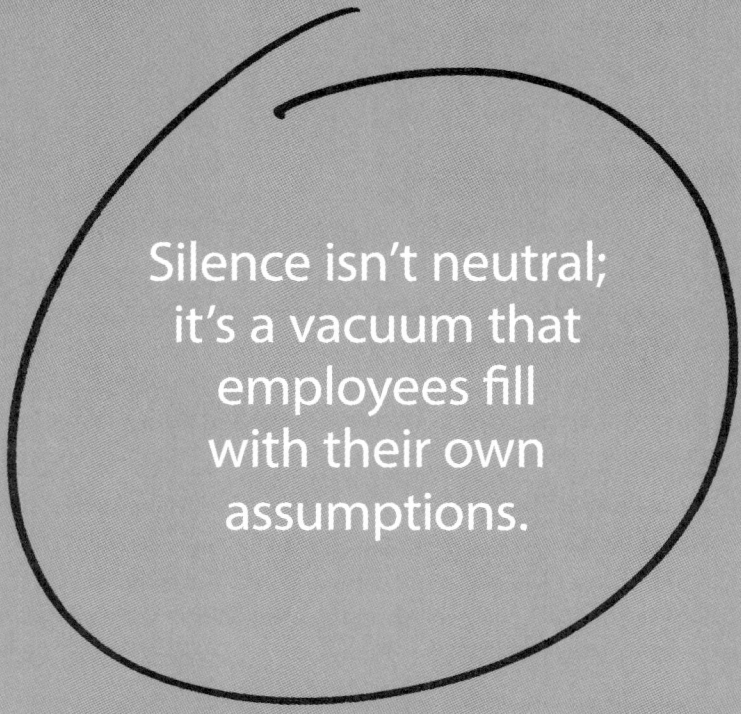

Silence isn't neutral;
it's a vacuum that
employees fill
with their own
assumptions.

AMPLIFY COMMUNICATION

Overcommunication is communication in the remote workplace.

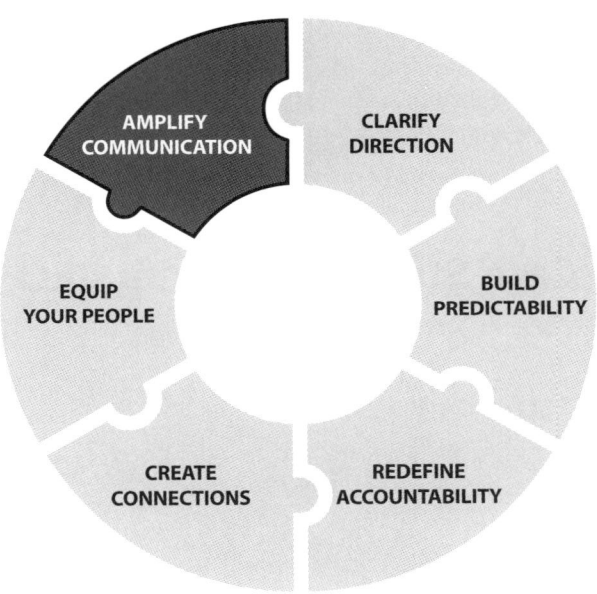

Communication—frequent, clear, and intentional—is the foundation of trust in a remote workplace. In traditional offices, trust is built in small, often unspoken moments: a reassuring smile in a hallway, a quick deskside chat to clarify a task, the natural energy of a group brainstorming session. But in remote work, those organic moments disappear.

If communication isn't intentional in the remote workplace, it doesn't happen. And when communication doesn't happen, assumptions, anxieties, and resentments fill the void:

Why didn't they respond to my email? Are they ignoring me? I wish I was more respected by this team.

That short message felt cold . . . what did I do to make her so upset with me?

No one clarified when this is due or how it should look. I guess I'll throw something together next week. That should be okay.

Missing information and an inability to turn to **supportive colleagues** to ask *"What is THAT all about?!"* make everything so much more complicated in the virtual workplace.

Case Study: The Silent CEO

A fully remote nonprofit organization that managed global environmental projects asked us for help. The CEO—a highly respected leader—had successfully led in-person teams for years. He prided himself on having an "open-door policy" and believed employees would reach out if they needed anything.

The problem?

He rarely initiated communication himself, was slow to respond to emails and texts, and hated learning new technology like intra-office messaging systems.

In the meetings he held with his team, it was obvious trouble was brewing. "Discussions" were filled with awkward silences, punctuated by occasional vague, self-promoting lectures by one of the newest directors. There was little energy, and very few decisions were made since the CEO didn't say much and team members were reluctant to offer opinions or volunteer to do extra work. The less the CEO said, the more the team disengaged, and

AMPLIFY COMMUNICATION

CLARIFY DIRECTION

BUILD PREDICTABILITY

REDEFINE ACCOUNTABILITY

CREATE CONNECTIONS

EQUIP YOUR PEOPLE

the quieter the meetings became. After a few months, the silence became deafening.

In reality, however, these meetings were anything but silent. The *real* frustrations were loudly shared, either during the meeting through covert direct messages (that did not include the CEO) or in end-of-day virtual "happy" hours (that really weren't very happy). The less communication there was from the leader, the greater the opportunity for each employee to create their own story:

What is really going on in this company? Why is the CEO failing to lead? Does he know something I don't know? Whose fault was that last team failure? It had better not be on me! How can I protect myself? I could do this so much better! Should I update my resume?

He rarely initiated communication himself, was slow to respond to emails and texts, and hated learning new technology like intra-office messaging systems.

Finally, during an in-person retreat, these frustrations boiled over. The employees weren't disengaged—they were **lost**. They had been operating in an **information void**, filled with assumptions, misunderstandings, and silent resentment. When the CEO heard their frustrations, he was stunned. He cared deeply about his team, but his passive approach had created confusion and distrust.

From that moment on, everything changed:

- The CEO scheduled weekly video check-ins—not just for tasks, but to personally connect with his team.

- He became more responsive, even to minor questions, reinforcing his presence as a leader.

- He started meetings with clarity, setting out the purpose, priorities, and expectations.

The takeaway? If you don't say it, people won't know it! Before we get into specific communication tools designed to increase online trust, take a minute to consider what you are already doing well and where your remote approach could use a little amplification.

Communication Benchmark Survey

How often do you engage in the following behaviors?

1. **Asking clarifying questions**

    1 = I think I need to get better at this.

    5 = I feel skilled at asking questions and tend to do it often.

    1   2   3   4   5

2. **Sending cryptic messages**

    1 = Yikes! I whip off short messages without proofreading all the time.

    5 = I feel pretty good about spelling ideas out in digital messages.

    1   2   3   4   5

3. **Ghosting people**

    1 = I am really bad at replying to emails.

    5 = I typically respond to all my emails in a timely manner.

    1   2   3   4   5

4. **Visually engaging in video meetings**

    1 = I almost always end up checking emails during video meetings. I guess people can tell.

    5 = I try hard to pay attention and maintain "eye contact" in video meetings.

    1   2   3   4   5

5. Giving grace

1 = When mistakes are made, I tend to assume the person is just not invested in doing the job.

5 = I'm pretty good at assuming good intentions.

1   2   3   4   5

6. What kind of communication do you think your employees wish you were better at?

Applying Your Results

Pay attention to your low scores. If you struggle with clarity, responsiveness, or assumptions, it's time to **amplify your communication.** We have six ideas to help you do just that.

AMPLIFY COMMUNICATION

CLARIFY DIRECTION

BUILD PREDICTABILITY

REDEFINE ACCOUNTABILITY

CREATE CONNECTIONS

EQUIP YOUR PEOPLE

The Six Keys to Amplified Communication

Remote communication isn't just about sending more messages—it's about ensuring the **right message** reaches the **right person** at the **right time** in the **right way**.

The best way to amplify communication is to focus on six key areas:

1. **Understanding:** Bridge the gaps caused by missing nonverbal cues.

2. **Respect:** Be intentional about digital etiquette and responsiveness.

3. **Information:** Proactively share updates to prevent confusion.

4. **Alignment:** Set norms and clarify expectations about communication channels.

5. **Curiosity:** Stop assuming and start asking more questions.

6. **Grace:** Give others the benefit of the doubt.

Understanding: Do Overcommunicate, Don't Underexplain

When the majority of nonverbal communication is missing, you need to provide more information.

Imagine this scenario. Lisa, a remote marketing manager, sends a quick email to her team: "We need the launch materials **ASAP**." To Lisa, it's obvious—this means it's urgent. She needs the materials *today*. But here's how her team interprets the message:

Jack: *ASAP means by the end of the week, right?*

Mira: *Does she mean just the graphics, or all the materials?*

Tom: *Wow. Lisa sounds angry. I wonder what THAT'S all about.*

Without clarity, everyone interprets the message differently. They don't have the luxury of all the context and nonverbal cues that might be available in an in-person office.

What might be a better approach?

To eliminate ambiguity, Lisa should be explicit: "We need the client proposal finalized by Thursday at 3 p.m. Eastern."

But what if her real issue is frustration over how long the team is taking to pull the proposal together? That's why she emphasized **ASAP** in the first place!

To Lisa, her emotions were clear. Unfortunately, reading emotion in virtual spaces never works like we think it does. Research from Oxford University suggests that when an individual believes they are *clearly* expressing outrage, frustration, or even sadness online, an **"illusion of transparency"** will result.[2] This illusion means that the sender might feel open, clear, and vulnerable in expressing themselves, while the virtually distant recipients have no idea there's anything emotional happening at all.

We can't expect our teams to accurately read our eye rolls on a video call or understand the frustrated intention of a bold **ASAP**

AMPLIFY COMMUNICATION

CLARIFY DIRECTION

BUILD PREDICTABILITY

REDEFINE ACCOUNTABILITY

CREATE CONNECTIONS

EQUIP YOUR PEOPLE

in a text. In our example, Lisa may need to actually bring the team together and *use words* to express her emotions:

"I'm frustrated with our progress . . ."

"I think we could do better . . ."

"I'm having trouble understanding . . ."

"I'm not sure I agree with our timeline . . ."

"This project has become overwhelming . . ."

"I'm excited to present this!"

To increase understanding in the remote workplace, we need to clarify both **content and emotion**.

✔ Virtual Tip

Use examples: The words we say need to be clear. Examples are a great way to clarify meaning. Make them specific and concrete. For example, if you would like your team to get better at anticipating the needs of their clients, *give an example* of how you saw someone actually anticipating a client's need.

Respect: Digital Body Language Matters

Every digital message has a tone—even if you didn't intend one.

Remote work introduces a whole new kind of body language.[3] Cues you might not have paid attention to before now hold profound meaning—cues like

- The speed of your reply
- The length of your response
- Your word choice and punctuation

Because there is so much missing nonverbal information in online environments, it's natural to search for *new* cues to help decipher meaning, intention, and emotion. Unfortunately, when you

AMPLIFY COMMUNICATION

CLARIFY DIRECTION

BUILD PREDICTABILITY

REDEFINE ACCOUNTABILITY

CREATE CONNECTIONS

EQUIP YOUR PEOPLE

send someone a short, error-ridden message, or take a long time to respond, or don't respond at all, you are sending a clear message that that person is simply not worth your time or energy.

Take, for example, how we communicate with the people who report to us. According to Erica Dhawan, author of *Digital Body Language*, "We may prioritize speed, clarity, and substantive messages with our bosses and clients but deliver one-liners with no subject lines to a junior report."[4] Unfortunately, those brief missives can be interpreted a thousand different ways:

"K"

"Fine."

"Not now."

"What??"

These kinds of responses leave our colleagues scratching their heads. They also loudly communicate a very important message:

You are not important enough for me to write an entire sentence.

And don't forget about timing. When a question is emailed, texted, or sent via the company's instant message platform, and you don't take the time to respond, you're not just withholding information—you're also loudly communicating another very important message:

I am too busy . . . for YOU.

 **Virtual Tip**

Respond positively:

- Acknowledge messages, even if you can't reply in full: "Great question—let me get back to you later this week."

- Consider adding a touch of warmth to responses that may be misinterpreted: "Thanks for this. I always appreciate your input."

Information: Prevent Siloed Communication

Information is only effective if it reaches the right people.

You may have heard comments like these:

"I didn't know that was happening. No one told *me!*"

"Was I supposed to be on that email?"

"I had no idea what that other team was doing. Turns out, we were working on the same thing!"

Silos pop up much more easily in the remote workplace. Information gets stuck when you don't run into people in the hall with updates or informally get caught up during lunch. In the remote office, individuals meet consistently with their team members, and for too many remote organizations, that's it. Unfortunately, that's when information sharing stops; what's happening in other parts of the organization simply gets lost in the deep virtual void.

In a remote workplace, don't assume people will naturally find out what they need to know. Strategically amplify important information so it is intentionally communicated to *everyone* who needs it.

 **Virtual Tip**

Communicate across teams:

- Schedule regular interdepartmental meetings and task each person to update their respective teams.
- Develop projects that include members from more than one department. By working together, teams get a broader view of what is happening in other silos.
- Take notes in meetings and post them to interdepartmental communication platforms.

Alignment: Set Clear Norms and Expectations

People don't just need direction—they want certainty.

Without in-person interactions, employees can't easily "read the room" to understand how work should be done. One way to establish expectations and reduce misunderstandings is to co-create a clear communication framework (see Table 1).

Table 1. The Virtual Communication Framework

Communication channels	What channels should we use for what purpose?	Intra-office messaging = quick questions
		Email = formal updates
		Video = strategy and intense or easily misunderstood discussions
Expected response time	How quickly should we respond?	Urgent = within 2 hours
		Routine = within 24 hours
Tone and format norms	How should we communicate?	Are emojis encouraged?
		How should subject lines be formatted? (Subject, urgency, response time, etc.)

Curiosity: Ask, Don't Assume

Don't let assumptions write your stories.

When working in remote and often isolated offices, it's easy to craft drama-filled novellas that help us make sense of incomplete information:

That message was really short . . . am I in trouble?

I can't believe she didn't finish the report like I asked . . . what's her problem?

The first step in identifying assumptions and seeking accurate information is to **interrupt the story**. We need to pay attention to the stories we are telling ourselves. The most compelling stories often pop up when we're trying to make sense of emotional or ambiguous comments, or when we feel like we are not quite qualified for a task or are being attacked. These are *exactly* the times we need to stop the storytelling and start the information seeking.

In their book *Difficult Conversations: How to Discuss What Matters Most*, Douglas Stone, Bruce Patton, and Sheila Heen refer to this changed mindset of seeking clarification as moving from **certainty to curiosity**. "For instance, instead of asking, 'How can they think that?!' try asking, 'I wonder what information they have that I don't?' or 'How might they see the world such that their view makes sense?'"

Certainty locks us out of their
story; curiosity lets us in.[5]

Case Study: Peggy's Misunderstood Colleague

This case is personal. One of my virtual coworkers—we'll call her Sarah—used to routinely make comments about how overworked she was. It was easy for me to feel resentful when I was doing essentially the same job, getting more done, and feeling just fine. It wasn't until we were on an in-person client retreat up in the snowy mountains of Colorado that I got information that changed my story.

At the end of a long, grueling day, we got to our team's condo, with a huge fireplace and moose-shaped cookies on the table. It was lovely, but I was so tired that I packed up my computer and went straight to bed. Sarah, on the other hand, stayed up another **three hours** organizing the notes from the day.

Over coffee the next morning, I asked her to tell me more about her late-night work session. She confessed that she never felt confident in these consulting situations and wanted to be as

AMPLIFY COMMUNICATION

CLARIFY DIRECTION

BUILD PREDICTABILITY

REDEFINE ACCOUNTABILITY

CREATE CONNECTIONS

EQUIP YOUR PEOPLE

prepared as possible. It helped her to get every last detail scripted and in place before walking into the room with the client. As she talked, I thought back to the many flawless presentations and detailed reports she had prepared over the years. I had to admit, they were beautiful. I had never stopped to think about the amount of **time** they had taken to prepare.

It was then that I realized something else. The off-the-cuff, "don't worry about it, we'll just go with the flow" way I approached my work probably overwhelmed Sarah. In fact, my mocking comments over dinner about her carefully crafted agenda had likely added another hour to her work the night before.

That extra piece of information about how my colleague approached stressful contexts, and how I contributed to her long days and nights, forced me to reevaluate the story I had been telling myself. My curiosity not only allowed me to understand Sarah better, but pushed me to **own my contribution** to the story. I also like to think the feedback I gave her on how well I thought she was doing and how much I appreciated her insights changed *her* story about her worth and about what it's like to work with me.

Curiosity rewrites stories. If we want to build trust at a distance, we need to ask the questions and have the hard conversations.

 Virtual Tip

Recognize context: Understand that people's actions can be influenced by factors you might not see. Everyone has a story.

Grace: Assume Good Intentions

It's easier to jump to negative conclusions than positive ones.

Assuming the worst comes naturally, especially when we're stressed or tired or feeling disconnected. Unfortunately, our minds are wired to focus on the negative; we tend to replay awkward or unflattering moments, obsessing over a single piece of criticism while overlooking a dozen compliments.

If we want grace from others, we must be ready to give it.

So how do we change our thinking? Before reacting, pause. That's it. Interrupt the storyline, then create a more positive plot:

They're probably really busy.

They might have misunderstood my request.

It doesn't seem like they're feeling well.

They haven't done this before; they may not know there's a better way to do it.

When we give our remote coworkers the benefit of the doubt—especially if we have a hunch that we are working with incomplete information—we have a chance at real communication, and real communication is the foundation for the development of real trust.

Final Thought: Be Intentional, Not Passive

Amplifying communication is not about adding more noise—it's about making sure the right messages reach the right people in the right way. That means no more passive, "open-door" policies. It means asking questions, paying attention, and checking assumptions. Decide how you are going to **intentionally** amplify communication with your team this week. Where will you begin?

- Understanding
- Respect
- Information
- Alignment
- Curiosity
- Grace

Trusted Leader Advice

Paige Hendrix Buckner, CEO of All Raise, an organization supporting women in the world of venture capital, shares some advice about the value of connecting: "Trust and clarity are the foundation of everything. This means clearly distinguishing between what needs synchronous attention (team meetings, one-on-ones, jam sessions, problem solving, emergencies, and tough conversations) versus what can be handled asynchronously (updates, FYIs, most decisions). It's important to model the vulnerability and boundaries you want to see. Effectiveness isn't about being available 24/7 but about delivering meaningful impact."[6]

AMPLIFY COMMUNICATION

CLARIFY DIRECTION

BUILD PREDICTABILITY

REDEFINE ACCOUNTABILITY

CREATE CONNECTIONS

EQUIP YOUR PEOPLE

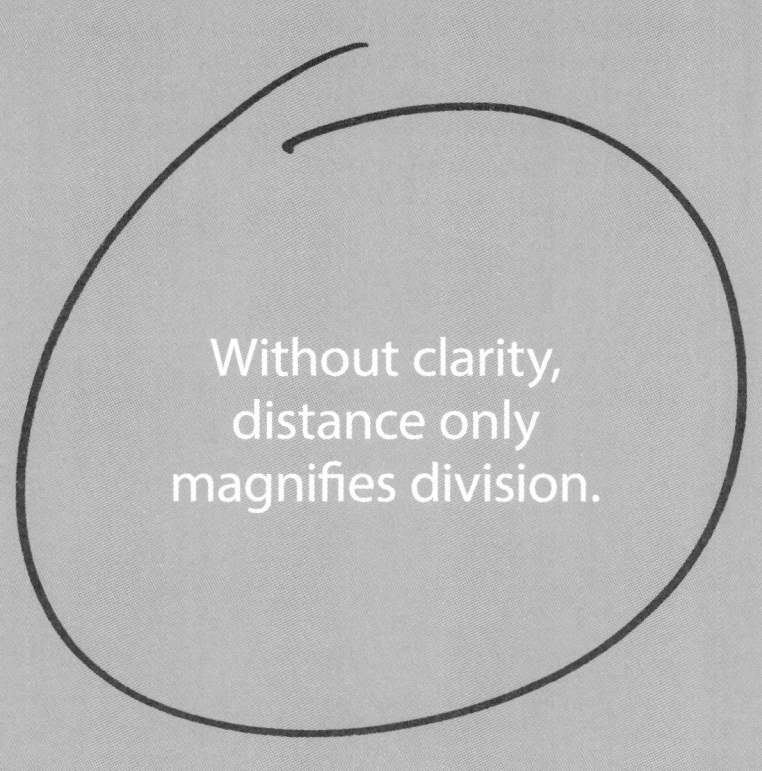

Without clarity,
distance only
magnifies division.

CLARIFY DIRECTION

Alignment is no longer a luxury.

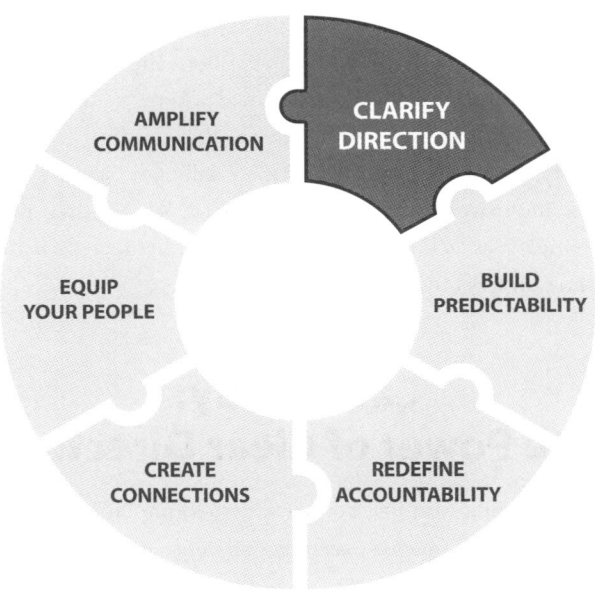

One of the greatest challenges of remote work is misalignment—a disconnect between employees' day-to-day tasks and the bigger mission of the organization. When employees are physically distant from leadership and their teams, it's far too easy for them to become disengaged and lose sight of what truly matters.

Without clear direction, a few outcomes result:

- **Employees drift.** They focus on tasks that seem urgent but may not contribute to larger goals.
- **Priorities compete.** Different teams pull in different directions, creating inefficiencies.
- **Trust erodes.** When people don't understand the "why" behind decisions, frustration builds.

That's why *clarifying direction* is the second key strategy to building trust at a distance. It's about ensuring both **big-picture clarity, where teams and** employees understand where the organization is going and how their work contributes to that mission, and **individual clarity,** where they know how their daily tasks align with key priorities and drive results. Both are essential: Without big-picture clarity, employees lack motivation; without individual clarity, they waste time on tasks that don't move the needle.

Case Study: The Power of Clear Direction

A national organization that connected emerging business leaders with high-powered finance executives and entrepreneurs had a problem. They had a talented team in place, but there was confusion about who was in charge, where the organization was going, and how they should all work together. Despite the organization's inspiring mission, employees felt lost.

Some of the problems included:

- **Confusing job roles:** No one was quite sure what they were responsible for.
- **Scattered leadership:** Employees received direction from multiple leaders but didn't know who had the final say or even who could ultimately fire them.

- **Lack of alignment:** Teams worked on overlapping projects without coordination.

- **No clear priorities:** Staff spent time on what *felt* important rather than what *was* important. Unfortunately, importance was defined differently by staff, volunteers, executives, and the board of directors.

Dealing with these kinds of challenges would have been hard in any context, but the remote nature of this workplace made it even more difficult. There were few opportunities for team members to address big-picture problems or ask for support and clarification from distant colleagues. When the CEO quit unexpectedly, the staff, who barely knew each other, were ready to flee.

At that moment, the organization faced a critical juncture. It needed strong leadership and clear direction. That's when a new interim CEO stepped in—**and everything changed**.

Turning Chaos into Clarity

From day one, the interim CEO took a radically different approach to leadership. She personally visited key volunteer groups across the country. She asked thoughtful questions, listened intently, and shared her vision, all while consistently updating and collaborating with her virtual team.

Then she did something even more powerful. Once the volunteer tour was complete, she brought the entire staff together for an in-person retreat. By the end of the gathering, they had co-created a unified vision, complete with streamlined workflows and clearly defined expectations:

- Together, they mapped out a new org chart, defined every role, and outlined the reporting structure. Employees no longer had to guess who made decisions or who was in charge.

AMPLIFY COMMUNICATION

CLARIFY DIRECTION

BUILD PREDICTABILITY

REDEFINE ACCOUNTABILITY

CREATE CONNECTIONS

EQUIP YOUR PEOPLE

- The leadership team established key organizational priorities. This helped employees focus on what mattered most rather than being pulled in different directions.

- Instead of letting confusion fester, the CEO held regular check-ins where employees could voice concerns and get answers.

The transformation was undeniable. The increased clarity and personal connection the interim CEO provided encouraged staff to begin to develop trust in their leader, her vision, each other, and ultimately the organization. As trust grew, employees slowly put away their resumes and replaced them with ideas for the company's future.

That's the power of clarity. When employees understand where the organization is going and how their work fits into the bigger picture, they don't just comply—they **commit**.

The Clarity Gap in Remote Work

This example highlights something critical: Clarity is harder to achieve in a remote environment.

In traditional offices, alignment happens more naturally. Employees overhear conversations and pick up on unspoken priorities based on who gets called into meetings, which projects get extra attention, and what ideas leaders emphasize or stress about in casual conversations.

In a virtual world, those natural touchpoints disappear. Instead, employees operate in individual silos, completing tasks in their isolated home offices, trying to make the best decisions they can with limited information. It's no wonder remote workers frequently report feeling disconnected from their company's mission and confused about how they fit in.

A Leadership Blind Spot

A common mistake remote leaders make is assuming, "Well, I told them once, so they must understand."

Not true. **Repetition is key.** Research shows that people need to hear a message at least seven times before they fully internalize it.[1]

In a remote environment, this means leaders must be far more intentional about reinforcing direction. It's not enough to mention priorities once in an email or a video town hall meeting. Leaders must consistently answer questions like

- What's most important *right now*?
- How does each employee's work contribute to the bigger picture?
- What decisions have been made—and why?

Without this level of clarity, employees will fill in the gaps with assumptions, misinterpretations, and personal priorities that may not align with company goals.

MVPs Are Crucial in Remote Work

A strong Mission, Values, and Priorities (MVP) framework isn't just a nice-to-have; it's essential in a remote work environment. Why? Because MVPs provide alignment, confidence, and a shared sense of purpose.

Let's break it down.

Mission: The WHY

A mission statement defines why the organization exists—what it is striving to achieve and what makes its work meaningful. The mission remains relatively unchanged over time and serves as the anchor that unites employees, no matter where they work.

AMPLIFY COMMUNICATION

CLARIFY DIRECTION

BUILD PREDICTABILITY

REDEFINE ACCOUNTABILITY

CREATE CONNECTIONS

EQUIP YOUR PEOPLE

For remote workers, a strong mission statement is even more critical because it prevents them from feeling like they're just checking off tasks in isolation. It connects their work to a larger, more inspiring purpose.

 **Virtual Tip**

Simplify the language:

- Use clear, concise, and relatable language in describing your mission. It ensures everyone understands, remembers, internalizes, and can easily explain the WHY behind what they are doing.

- Begin the mission statement with "To," making sure it is action oriented. Take for example, the mission statement of Starbucks: "To be the premier purveyor of the finest coffee in the world, inspiring and nurturing the human spirit— one person, one cup and one neighborhood at a time."[2]

Values: The WAY

Values define how the organization operates, makes decisions, and interacts with employees, customers, and partners. They serve as the ethical and cultural foundation of the company, providing a framework for behavior and decision making.

In an in-person setting, company values are often absorbed naturally, through leadership actions, team dynamics, and office interactions. However, remote workers don't have the luxury of seeing how people react when they think no one is looking. Clear and authentic organizational values help remote workers understand what is expected from them and provide guidance on how the team culture works, what behavior is encouraged, and what should be avoided.

Case Study: The Late Marketing Team

A fully remote marketing agency had one major problem: It struggled with employees missing deadlines.

As the leaders strategized about how they could motivate employees to do a better job, they discussed a whole array of punishments and threats, feeling uncomfortable with how each option might impact trust.

It was then that the CEO brought up the company's values. They decided it was time to emphasize the value of "extreme ownership." This value was all about taking personal responsibility.

Leaders became intentional about using the phrase, referencing it in some way in almost every meeting. Wins were celebrated that exemplified the value, and decisions and feedback were explicitly tied to how well the project aligned with personal accountability and ownership.

It wasn't long before deadlines started being made. This didn't happen because employees were echoing the words; they actually started *adopting the value*. For instance, they created a shared document where they openly tracked deadlines, updated progress, and took personal accountability. "Extreme ownership" became part of every project and every task. Slowly, the culture shifted from frustration to responsibility—all without micromanaging or losing trust.

Values can impact expectations, satisfaction, and behavior. **Intentional communication of those values is required in the remote workplace.** Without clear repetition, definitions, rewards, and stories, these ideals will get lost in the remote distance.

 **Virtual Tip**

> **Check out your values:** Ask employees what they think your company values are—not what's on the website, but what they actually experience. If there's a gap, it's time to realign.

Priorities: The HOW

Priorities are the bridge between mission and daily work. They guide strategic focus and decision making, ensuring that employees don't just stay busy—they stay productive in what actually matters.

In remote settings, where employees don't have as much visibility into leadership decisions, well-communicated priorities are a *lifeline*. Without them, teams can become fragmented, focusing on different goals or working at cross-purposes.

Case Study: A Global Priority

A global tech startup had teams in multiple time zones. Without clear priorities, employees were feeling overwhelmed, unsure whether they should be focusing on product development, customer support, or internal process improvements. When different leaders and different teams ended up focusing on different priorities, productivity and morale swiftly fell.

To fix this, the CEO implemented a weekly **"Top 3"** update. Every Monday, they sent out an email outlining the three most important priorities for the week. Teams then aligned their work accordingly and discussed roadblocks during their weekly check-ins.

This simple practice increased productivity, reduced confusion, and gave employees confidence in their decision making.

 **Virtual Tip**

> **Seek alignment:** Encourage employees to ask themselves: *Is what I'm working on today aligned with my top priorities, and do I know how they relate to the company's priorities?* If they can't answer that question easily, the organizational priorities may not be clear.

The most effective remote teams don't just do work—they understand the **WHY, WAY, and HOW** behind it. When leaders take the time to clarify and reinforce direction, remote employees feel more confident, more connected, and more engaged.

Consider creating an MVP framework (see Table 2).

Table 2. The MVP Framework

MVP ELEMENT	PURPOSE	WHY IT MATTERS IN REMOTE WORK
Mission (WHY)	Defines the organization's purpose	Keeps remote employees connected to the bigger picture
Values (WAY)	Guides decision making and behavior	Creates consistency across dispersed teams
Priorities (HOW)	Focuses time, energy, and resources	Helps employees make independent decisions that align with company goals

AMPLIFY COMMUNICATION

CLARIFY DIRECTION

BUILD PREDICTABILITY

REDEFINE ACCOUNTABILITY

CREATE CONNECTIONS

EQUIP YOUR PEOPLE

Direction Benchmark Survey

Before diving into action steps, let's take a moment to assess where you currently stand in clarifying and communicating your organization's direction.

1. **How clear are your organization's Mission, Values, and Priorities (MVPs)?**

   1 = I think I know what they are . . . aren't they on the website somewhere?

   5 = Our Mission, Values, and Priorities are easy to remember and guide our daily work.

   1   2   3   4   5

2. **How often do you talk about organizational MVPs?**

   1 = I almost never mention our MVPs—do we even have those?

   5 = I regularly remind team members of our Mission, Values, and Priorities in meetings and conversations.

   1   2   3   4   5

3. **How often do you tell stories that promote your MVPs?**

   1 = I tell a lot of stories—but I rarely tie them back to the MVPs.

   5 = I regularly share stories of how we are making an impact.

   1   2   3   4   5

4. **How involved is your team in crafting organizational strategy?**

   1 = The executives put the org strategy together. I'm not exactly sure what it is, and I don't think employees know that we even have one.

   5 = We meet regularly to review and refine our organization's strategy, gathering input from as many employees and stakeholders as possible.

   1   2   3   4   5

Applying Your Results

If you scored below 3 on any of these questions, it's time to revisit your MVPs. Are they still relevant? Do they need to be reintroduced? If you don't have a direct role in crafting them, who can you speak with about making them more visible and actionable? The answer to question 4 is crucial. If employees aren't part of the strategic direction-setting process, you may find building trust will take even more time and energy than you originally planned.

AMPLIFY COMMUNICATION

CLARIFY DIRECTION

BUILD PREDICTABILITY

REDEFINE ACCOUNTABILITY

CREATE CONNECTIONS

EQUIP YOUR PEOPLE

Four Ways to Strengthen Alignment in a Remote Workplace

When employees understand where they're going and why their work matters, they don't just follow orders—they become **fully engaged contributors.** A well-crafted strategic plan does little good unless it is integrated into everyday decisions and conversations within the organization.

The following are four proven ways to build trust at a distance by reinforcing your Mission, Values, and Priorities:

1. Conversations

2. Repetition

3. Stories

4. Goal alignment

Build Direction into Everyday Conversations

Work toward making conversations about MVPs both normal and comfortable. For example:

- **When reviewing an idea:** "That's a great suggestion! Let's discuss how it fits into our mission."

- **When recognizing great work:** "The way you handled that client aligns perfectly with our value of 'Integrity in every interaction.'"

- **When prioritizing tasks:** "Which of these projects best supports our top company priorities? Let's focus on that first."

✔ Virtual Tip

Use quick reminders: If your team meets over video, start each meeting with a one-minute highlight of a company value or a short example of how it's been recently demonstrated.

Repeat, Repeat, Repeat

People forget. It's essential to repeat your MVPs in multiple formats, without sounding forced or robotic. Here are some suggestions:

- Start board, committee, or staff meetings with a quick MVP reminder.

- Include an MVP reference in email signatures, internal messaging channels, videoconferencing backgrounds, or organizational dashboards.

- Use asynchronous tools (internal messaging, newsletters, recorded video updates) to reinforce key messages between live meetings.

- Begin every leadership meeting by asking each department to share one way they advanced the company's mission that week.

✔ Virtual Tip

Let MVPs drive decision making: Use the Mission, Values, and Priorities as an explicit framework for decisions and problem solving. This will not only help ensure your decisions stay aligned but make decision making faster and more efficient.

Use Stories to Reinforce Direction

Facts inform. Stories inspire.

People don't remember corporate jargon—but they remember stories. Stories make MVPs real by showing employees what success in action looks like.

Case Study: A Storytelling Banker

A regional bank president understood the power of storytelling. Because he couldn't physically be in every branch for every staff meeting, he instituted a company-wide policy: Every staff meeting should end with someone sharing an example of how an employee

AMPLIFY COMMUNICATION

CLARIFY DIRECTION

BUILD PREDICTABILITY

REDEFINE ACCOUNTABILITY

CREATE CONNECTIONS

EQUIP YOUR PEOPLE

had made a difference that week—whether it was a teller who helped an elderly customer navigate online banking or a loan officer who saved a small business from closing. The most powerful stories were then saved and shared at a year-end reward celebration, where the entire organization was reminded of how every team member played a role in fulfilling the bank's mission.

David's Personal Storytelling Lesson

The power of storytelling is something that has become central to how I lead. I had the privilege of being mentored by Don Soderquist, COO of Walmart for over two decades. Don was instrumental in taking Walmart from a $1 billion company to one with yearly revenues of over $200 billion. Started by Sam Walton and carried on by Don and other senior leaders, the Saturday Morning Meeting—a weekly gathering of leaders near Walmart's corporate offices—was a structured, much-anticipated opportunity to share ideas and stories. It helped cement MVPs into the everyday culture of Walmart. According to Don, it was during one of these Saturday meetings that a leader shared the story of a beautiful experience they'd had the week before, when an employee had gone out of their way to greet their wheelchair-bound friend. Don was so moved by this story that he introduced the role of "greeter" in Walmart stores across the country.[3]

Stories bring the Mission, Values, and Priorities to life.

 **Virtual Tip**

> **Recognize contributions:** Publicly celebrate employees who demonstrate a strong commitment to your mission and values. Keep a shared document or internal messaging channel where team members can share and celebrate short "**mission moments**."

Align Individual and Team Goals with MVPs

Your employees should never have to guess how their work contributes to company success. One of the simplest ways to create alignment is to connect team and individual goals to the company's MVPs. This can be achieved in a number of ways, including:

- Quarterly objectives and key results (OKRs) that reflect company priorities

- Team goals that flow directly from long-term strategic objectives

- Weekly priorities that explicitly reinforce core values

At Trust Edge Leadership Institute, we use a simple tool called **Priority Alignment**.[4] It works like this:

- If a company's priorities are A, B, and C, then every employee needs to know which priority their work supports—A, B, and/or C.

- Some team members will focus entirely on one goal, while others balance two.

This visual alignment exercise (Figure 1) prevents wasted effort on tasks that don't contribute to top priorities.

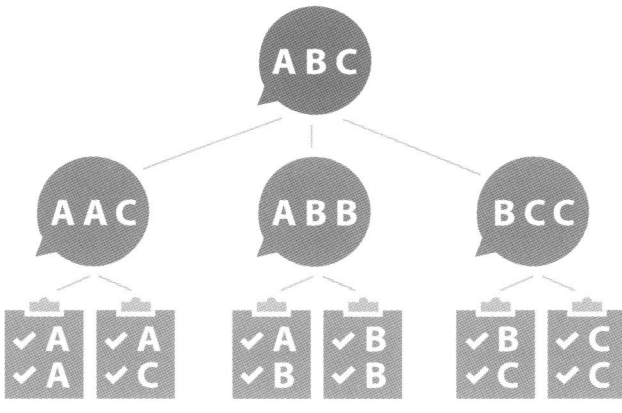

Figure 1. Priority Alignment

AMPLIFY COMMUNICATION

CLARIFY DIRECTION

BUILD PREDICTABILITY

REDEFINE ACCOUNTABILITY

CREATE CONNECTIONS

EQUIP YOUR PEOPLE

 **Virtual Tip**

Provide consistent reinforcement: In your regular one-on-one check-ins, discuss with employees how their work aligns with the company or team's MVPs.

The Power of Getting in the Same Room

We know this book is about creating trust at a distance, but we've also seen the power of in-person experiences, especially related to clarifying direction. If possible, consider getting employees together in real life to co-create or assess the organization's MVPs. This process can have several important outcomes:

- It creates space for authentic, naturally flowing conversations related to the Mission, Values, and Priorities, further cementing the shared vision for the future.

- It enables the creation of strategy informed by input from across the organization, boosting ownership and engagement.

- It strengthens relationships, making virtual collaboration even more effective after the event.

Whether it's a three-day annual retreat or a quarterly one-day brainstorming session, when you gather everyone together in one place, isolated, remote employees will have the opportunity to physically reengage and feel valued for their ability to contribute to the organization's mission.

✔ **Virtual Tip**

Incorporate "double-loop" feedback: Make sure to let employees know how their feedback and ideas are being implemented. This keeps everyone in the loop and reminds them that you really are listening.

Final Thought:
Clarity Drives Trust

At a distance, clarity about direction isn't optional—it's essential. When employees understand the mission, they feel purpose. When they embrace the values, they make better decisions. When they know the priorities, they focus on what truly matters.

The more clearly leaders communicate direction, the more remote employees will trust that their work is meaningful, aligned, and valued.

> ## Trusted Leader Advice
>
> Nate Regier, CEO of Next Element Consulting, highlights the importance of Mission, Values, and Priorities in a remote workplace: "We have a clear process for documenting strategic goals and deliverables, and a dedicated 'Visionary' role to keep the vision front and center. Remote workers especially crave a unifying purpose that guides them toward where the organization is headed."[5]

AMPLIFY COMMUNICATION

CLARIFY DIRECTION

BUILD PREDICTABILITY

REDEFINE ACCOUNTABILITY

CREATE CONNECTIONS

EQUIP YOUR PEOPLE

In remote work,
silence never
speaks reassurance.

BUILD PREDICTABILITY

Consistent points of contact
combat virtual uncertainty.

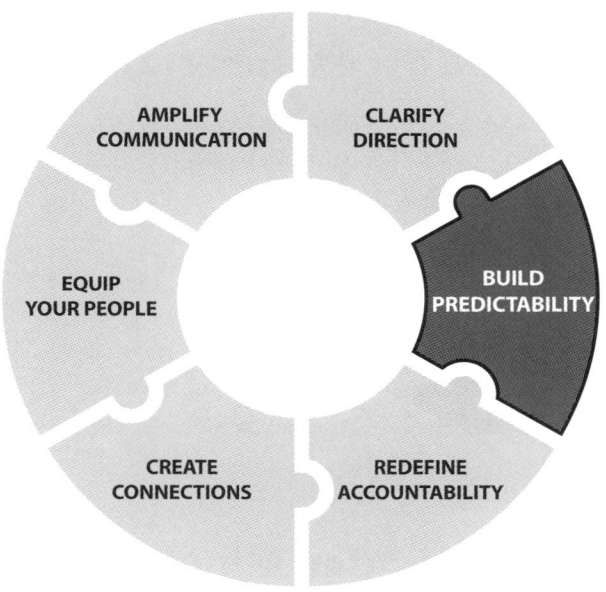

Today, unpredictability is certain. With changing technologies, shifting politics, and the pendulum swinging from one type of workplace to another, leaders are often left feeling confused, off-balance, and, well, just a little bit tired. Change is inevitable, and adapting is hard.

Remember the first day of your last job? You might not have actually accomplished much (except smiling a lot), but chances are you were exhausted by the end of the day. Everything was new;

nothing was predictable. You had to think about *everything all at once*. But as time passed, you started to figure it out. You picked up on the unwritten rules, the subtle office dynamics, and the informal ways people got work done. Eventually, you knew which tasks were urgent, what made your manager happy, and what kinds of jokes were safe to make in the break room. You were able to decipher the *implicit* expectations behind the *explicit* directions. The more predictable your day became, the more you were able to relax.

The Cost of Uncertainty

In a perfect world, this kind of learning takes place naturally and over time. You can quietly observe and learn, without too many colleagues knowing when you are feeling more like an imposter than an expert. That is not the case in the remote office. There are few opportunities to watch people to learn the subtle expectations of the team. When you have to ask for help, everyone knows it. When changes occur, you may not see the warning signs, so you're never quite certain about what might be coming next.

Unfortunately, the impact of too much uncertainty is always increased anxiety, exhaustion, and burnout.

The Hidden Minefields of Remote Work

A lack of predictability in any workplace is stressful. But in a remote setting, it can feel like navigating a minefield full of unseen dangers.

Think about some of the accidental mines you have detonated at work. Maybe things like

- Referring to a senior colleague by their first name instead of "Dr.," and watching everyone look up to enjoy the inevitable blowback

- Making a small joke about the CEO during a meeting, only to be met with dead silence

- Sending a friendly emoji in an email to a client, only to find out later "Um, this company doesn't emoji"

The worst thing about landmines is that you don't know where the danger lies. However, if you have a map of where the landmines are buried, you have a reasonable chance of staying safe. You don't have to worry as much because you know where *not* to step. Work patterns become easier, and you know that your relationships won't be blown apart at any minute because now you know what to avoid. The more certainty you have, the safer you feel. **When people feel secure, trust thrives.**

A Simple Yet Critical Tool

The single most predictable behavior in successful remote organizations is the use of consistent check-ins.

We have learned an important lesson from working with remote organizations: There is a cost associated with haphazard or nonexistent points of contact:

- When employees don't have regular access to leaders, they make assumptions.

- When they don't have time to ask questions, they hold those questions in while frustration and feelings of confusion and abandonment build.

- When feedback is delayed, projects veer off course.

Without intentional check-ins, remote employees end up working in the dark, figuring out the answers to their questions on their own without guidance or reassurance. This is a recipe for reduced morale, disengagement, and declining trust in leadership.

AMPLIFY COMMUNICATION

CLARIFY DIRECTION

BUILD PREDICTABILITY

REDEFINE ACCOUNTABILITY

CREATE CONNECTIONS

EQUIP YOUR PEOPLE

Predictability Benchmark Survey

Take a moment to assess the current level of structured communication and predictability.

1. **What are your team's predictable rhythms?**

   What regular activities or check-ins do your employees count on?

   How do they know when you'll be available to answer questions?

2. **My employees can count on meeting with me regularly.**

   1 = We don't have anything formal set up.

   5 = It's regular. Like clockwork. They can count on me.

   1   2   3   4   5

3. **How often do you cancel check-ins?**

   1 = When we get busy, check-ins are usually the first thing to go.

   5 = I schedule them, and I show up. Period.

   1   2   3   4   5

4. **My employees have clear and consistent channels to ask questions.**

   1 = Hmm. Not sure. I think they just work it out.

   5 = We have regular check-ins and an agreed-upon channel for questions between meetings.

   1   2   3   4   5

5. My check-ins are effective.

    1 = They feel like a waste of time. Honestly, I try to avoid them.

    5 = They're quick, regular, and valuable.

1   2   3   4   5

Applying Your Results

If you gave yourself less than a 4 on any of these survey questions, you've just identified one of the most effective ways to start building trust in your team:

- If you can't identify clear daily or weekly rhythms, start with one simple check-in with your team each week. See what happens.
- If your check-ins are sporadic or inconsistent, choose a recurring time and stick to it.
- If check-ins seem ineffective, adjust the structure—ask more open-ended questions, encourage updates, and provide actionable feedback.

The next section will explore how to create effective check-ins, set clear expectations, and remove uncertainty from remote workflows—because when employees know what to expect, they feel more confident, engaged, and connected.

AMPLIFY COMMUNICATION

CLARIFY DIRECTION

BUILD PREDICTABILITY

REDEFINE ACCOUNTABILITY

CREATE CONNECTIONS

EQUIP YOUR PEOPLE

The "Figure It Out" Trap

At Trust Edge Leadership Institute, one of our core values is "figure it out." It's meant to empower autonomy and encourage problem solving. But in remote work settings, we've seen how this value can be stretched too far—morphing into what we call the "figure it out" trap.

Instead of being empowered, employees begin to feel isolated and unsure. With no support, confidence in their decisions fades, and they're left wondering whether their work aligns with broader company goals.

You may have heard this sentiment from remote colleagues:

I'm not even sure my manager knows what I do every day. The only time we talk is when there's a problem.

Trust isn't just about letting people work **independently**—it's about ensuring they feel **supported** and **connected**.

The "Open Door" Myth

Another pitfall we see in remote offices has to do with doors. The in-person office has all sorts of symbolic ways of communicating important messages. For instance, we know that when a leader's door is closed, it means they're too busy to talk. When it's open, this alerts employees that they can stop by and ask questions. Some leaders even put out candy jars or display family pictures to encourage socializing and draw people in through their open door. Doors make it easy. Employees know how, when, and where to get information or check in.

Reality check: An open-door policy doesn't work when there are no doors.

In the remote office, employees can't see the door position, and they can't tell when is a good time to talk. When there is no additional information, the default assumption will always be that the virtual door is closed. And here's the problem: If the boss always seems too busy to talk, then there's never a good time to ask a quick question or voice a growing concern. That, in turn, communicates "you are on your own" as loudly as if the physical office door were locked up tight.

One thing we have clearly heard from remote workers is that they usually won't take the initiative to reach out unless they're in trouble.

Rather than waiting for employees to come to you, **you need to open the door**. Proactively scheduling check-ins and creating a culture where questions, feedback, and updates happen on a predictable basis is the only way to let people know when your virtual door is *actually open*.

 **Virtual Tip**

Become accessible: Establish "office hours" at specific times during the week where you will work online in a videoconferencing "room." This will allow employees to pop in and ask quick questions.

Check-Ins: The Nonnegotiable Habit of High-Trust Teams

Creating predictability through regular check-ins is one of the **most effective ways** to build trust at a distance. But how do you make them efficient, impactful, and sustainable?

There are three key elements to keep in mind:

1. **Time:** Make space for check-ins despite busy schedules.

2. **Consistency:** Keep them reliable and predictable.

3. **Structure:** Ensure they are focused and valuable.

Time: The ROI on Check-Ins

I'm too busy for this!

Many leaders feel that adding more meetings—especially one-on-ones—is too time-consuming. But the reality is that *not* checking in costs more in the long run. Here's why:

- Misaligned expectations create rework.

- Lack of feedback leads to poor performance.

- Unanswered questions cause delays and inefficiencies.

- All of these challenges destroy trust.

According to a 2023 Gallup poll, 80 percent of employees who said they'd had "meaningful conversations" with a supervisor in the past week reported that they were **fully engaged**—*regardless of whether they worked remotely.*[1] Keep in mind that a "meaningful conversation" isn't necessarily a long, all-consuming session. It can be a quick, focused interaction that includes recognition, appreciation, collaboration, relationship building, or clarification of current goals and priorities.

Many leaders find that a weekly fifteen-minute meeting is enough to meet employees' most urgent needs, ensuring alignment without overwhelming schedules.

But what if my calendar is already full?

Try it out. Commit to practicing weekly check-ins with each direct report for ninety days. The first couple of meetings may go long, but you'll become more efficient over time. You may decide to have ten-minute weekly check-ins and longer monthly debriefs for concerns you don't have time to cover each week. The key is maintaining a consistent rhythm.

 Virtual Tip

Use small group check-ins: By meeting regularly with a small group, along with weekly or bimonthly one-on-ones, you can accomplish many of the same goals of engagement, alignment, and information sharing *and* save time.

Consistency: Show Up Every Time

If you say you're going to meet . . . then meet!

One of the biggest mistakes leaders make is canceling check-ins at the last minute. Each time a leader cancels a one-on-one, they send a message:

You're not a priority.

Figure it out on your own.

I don't have time for you.

Peggy's Personal Case Study: The Impact of Check-Ins

Early in my career, I worked for a leader who emphasized mentorship and teamwork. I was excited to be part of a culture that prioritized leadership development and was anxious to learn new skills and improve the areas of expertise I already had.

But over time, I noticed a pattern: the meetings I scheduled with the CEO were frequently canceled. I often found myself in a virtual meeting room alone, wondering if the leader was going to show up. As more and more check-ins were canceled, usually at the last minute, it became apparent that I wasn't as important as I had thought. It was clear I was going to have to figure this job out on my own if I was going to be successful. I was forced to enter client meetings feeling unprepared, and with every project, I felt less confident in my skills and more stressed about my ability to handle the unknown.

The hardest part was the emotional toll. There's nothing like sitting in an empty digital room, knowing you've been forgotten. Feelings of uncertainty, marginalization, and frustration had time and opportunity to take hold as I waited in those lonely virtual spaces, and it eventually led to disengagement and an unwillingness to volunteer or add my ideas to future projects.

Then it all changed. Hard conversations were had, and an experienced consultant stepped in and committed to weekly meetings—**no matter what**. At first, I used those sessions to ask all my

AMPLIFY COMMUNICATION

CLARIFY DIRECTION

BUILD PREDICTABILITY

REDEFINE ACCOUNTABILITY

CREATE CONNECTIONS

EQUIP YOUR PEOPLE

pent-up questions. But as time went on, my trust in my colleague grew, and I found that I had fewer questions to ask. I started using the extra few minutes of each call to connect. I'd ask about difficult client situations; she would encourage and empower me. We would laugh about our stumbles and cheer our successes.

Over time, something remarkable happened: Our team became an actual team. I gained confidence and got better at my job. **Short and consistent**, that's all those check-ins were. But they reduced stress, cultivated connection, and built a lasting trust.

 ## Virtual Tip

Lead by example:

- Be punctual, prepared, and fully present during check-ins.
- Maintain the priority so you don't feel tempted to cancel.
- Model the tone and level of engagement you expect from others.

Structure: Keep it Simple

But I run out of things to say . . .

Some leaders avoid check-ins because they don't know how to structure them. The solution? **A simple, repeatable agenda.**

A Proven Framework for Check-Ins

Try these four simple questions for one-on-one or team check-ins:

1. What can we celebrate?
2. What are your priorities for the week?
3. What are your biggest challenges for accomplishing those goals?
4. How can I help?

AMPLIFY COMMUNICATION

CLARIFY DIRECTION

BUILD PREDICTABILITY

REDEFINE ACCOUNTABILITY

CREATE CONNECTIONS

EQUIP YOUR PEOPLE

Case Study: A Predictable Win

Jean was an executive in a large healthcare system and found herself in charge of a new team. She knew she had to make changes, as the team was recovering from a leader who had created chaos and instability every time he logged on. Jean decided to schedule regular meetings with each team member, using a structured set of questions each week. As time passed, she noticed her employees became used to the questions and would arrive prepared with answers. As a result, the information gathering part of the check-ins grew much more efficient.

The unexpected benefit came at the end of each of these meetings. Employees began trusting Jean enough to open up about parts of their lives they normally would have had little opportunity to share—whether it was news of a child graduating from high school, discussion of the challenges of caring for an aging parent, or excitement about a new idea they'd come up with. This, in turn, made them feel they had a safe space to come to when they had a particularly difficult or embarrassing issue to discuss.

Jean felt that the positive nature of her questions also helped shift the tone of the entire culture. Employees knew she would publicly recognize the good work being identified in those meetings, and they became more comfortable celebrating team wins.

A final unexpected benefit happened when Jean started keeping records of the issues being raised by employees. With this information, she was able to track the rise of specific concerns—and when she met with her supervisors, she had clear evidence to support her recommendations and conclusions. Without a doubt, regular check-ins were the key to building trust in this organization.

 **Virtual Tip**

Follow up after one-on-ones: Summarize key takeaways, action items, and next steps in a shared document or email. Track progress on discussed items in subsequent check-ins to show follow-through.

Beyond Individual Meetings: Creative Ways to Build Predictability

Building predictable routines is done differently in every organization. Here are some ideas for raising the level of your check-in game:

- **Work partners:** Ask employees to pair up and have a daily ten-minute video call with one other person to share their top three priorities for the day.

- **Monday kickoff meetings:** Start each week with a teamwide check-in on goals and anticipated challenges for the week.

- **End-of-day check-ins:** Have employees send a one-phrase summary of their day in the company's internal chat as they are logging off for the day.

- **Predictable rhythms:** Have daily "stand-up" team meetings to start each day, weekly video calls with the team and the CEO, monthly team meetups (say, lunch at a local restaurant), and quarterly one-on-one employee–supervisor meetings.

Final Thought: Predictability Creates Trust

Leaders who create predictable rhythms of connection build trust, alignment, and high-performing teams. If you're looking for a good first step to build trust at a distance, scheduling regular check-ins is a great place to start.

Trusted Leader Advice

Eric Mahler, Fortune 500 advisor and cofounder of Alpine Wolf Capital, has found that in remote work, interaction needs to be much more frequent: "With a remote or hybrid team, use daily kick-off or Scrum calls.[2] These get people online right away in the morning for fifteen to thirty minutes to synchronize efforts and to provide updates. Daily communication keeps everyone working in the same direction and has been a real game changer."[3]

AMPLIFY COMMUNICATION

CLARIFY DIRECTION

BUILD PREDICTABILITY

REDEFINE ACCOUNTABILITY

CREATE CONNECTIONS

EQUIP YOUR PEOPLE

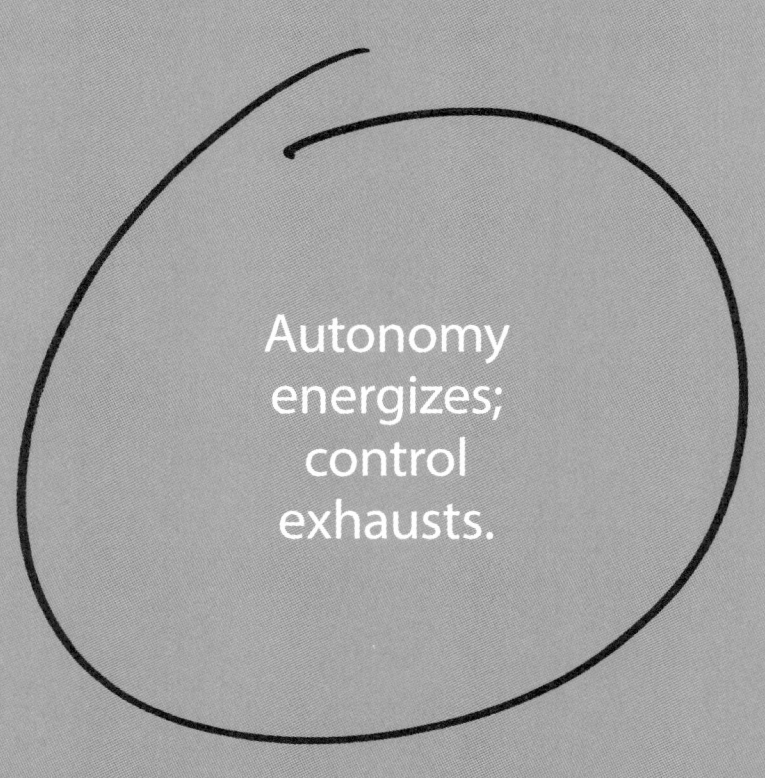

Autonomy
energizes;
control
exhausts.

REDEFINE ACCOUNTABILITY

Ditch the time clock and
embrace accountable autonomy.

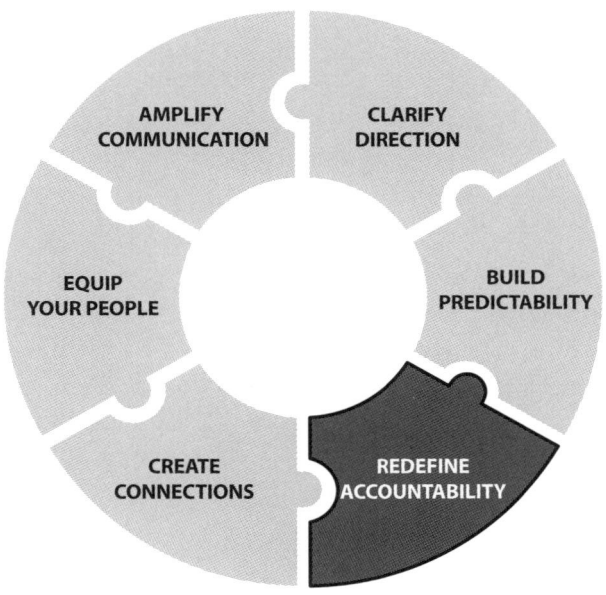

As the modern workplace embraces remote and hybrid work arrangements, many leaders struggle with concerns about employee productivity. Without the ability to observe who arrives early or who appears busy at their desk, it's common for remote managers to wonder whether distributed team members are really doing what they were hired to do.

The Remote Work Dilemma:
Trust Versus Control

During the COVID-19 pandemic, leaders adjusting to the remote workplace were often suspicious of their remote employees, questioning whether they were truly working or just collecting paychecks.

Take the case of Vishal Garg, the CEO of Better.com, who made headlines when he gathered 900 employees on a three-minute Zoom call—only to fire them all immediately. His reasoning? As he told his managers, "At least 250 of the people terminated were working an average of two hours a day while clocking in eight. They were stealing from you and stealing from our customers. Get educated."[1]

Or consider Molly, an instructional designer featured on the business podcast *Marketplace*. She got a part-time job working from home, then landed a second full-time remote job—and decided to keep them both. Using two laptops labeled with sticky notes, she managed overlapping meetings by keeping her camera on for one and her microphone on for the other, following social cues to appear engaged in both. She admitted, "It's like being an actress."[2]

It would be nice to think that these are simply extreme cases, but evidence suggests the misuse of remote work flexibility is more common than we think:

- In 2023, the #overemployed hashtag, representing those working more than one remote job at a time, had over 4.3 million views on TikTok.[3]

- The r/overemployed Reddit group had over 99,000 members, ranking in the top 1 percent of all Reddit communities by size.[4]

- Online forums are filled with tips and tricks for holding multiple remote jobs at once and circumventing employee monitoring tools.

For many leaders, stories like these confirm their worst fears: *If I can't see my employees, are they REALLY working?*

The "Big Brother" Response

From the earliest days of organized workplaces, there has been an uneasy relationship between employee autonomy and organizational accountability. The work-from-home office has only magnified the struggle leaders face as they try to supervise from a distance. As a result, some organizations have turned to extreme surveillance to regain control, using tactics and products such as

- Mouse movement trackers to detect inactivity
- Randomized screenshot apps to monitor screens
- Live webcam monitoring software to watch employees work
- Keystroke loggers for constant, undetected oversight
- Web browsing monitors to track online behavior
- Time-tracking software measuring productivity down to the minute

On the surface, these kinds of monitoring approaches may seem like a simple solution to bridging the remote work trust gap. But research shows *they usually backfire*. A study out of the University of Wyoming suggests that digital surveillance by supervisors often produces the exact opposite of the intended effect, with a "moral disengagement" occurring when employees feel so clearly distrusted.[5] This often translates into a lack of remorse as these disempowered employees actively engage in finding ways to cheat the monitoring systems.

A psychological toll is exacted when employees are micromanaged. The result is a workforce that is less engaged, less innovative, and much more resentful.

AMPLIFY COMMUNICATION

CLARIFY DIRECTION

BUILD PREDICTABILITY

REDEFINE ACCOUNTABILITY

CREATE CONNECTIONS

EQUIP YOUR PEOPLE

A Better Way: Accountable Autonomy

Instead of relying on **blind trust** or **overbearing surveillance**, successful remote organizations adopt something we call *accountable autonomy*:

Accountability + Autonomy = Accountable Autonomy

Accountable autonomy flows from a trusting relationship. It maximizes **employee autonomy and expertise** while embedding **accountability practices** into the culture of the organization.

Accountable autonomy allows employees to gain freedom over how they work, building motivation, ownership, and creativity, all while promoting alignment and results.

The Opportunity of Autonomy

One of the clearest benefits to remote work is that employees gain more control over how they go about their work, including what they do and when they do it. Of course, *more* control for the employee automatically results in *less* control for the organization. That's not always an easy ask. So, before we discuss how to adopt this new brand of **employee accountability**, it's important to look at the many benefits of **employee autonomy**.

Autonomy Brings Out the Best in People

We know that positive relationships are key to a healthy workplace culture. But as those relationships become more dispersed, a feeling of anonymity naturally grows. Research consistently shows that this can bring out both the worst *and* the best in people.

Too much anonymity can embolden people to act in hurtful and thoughtless ways, often without facing consequences. But that same anonymity can also set individuals free to be the **best version of themselves**. For instance, a 2010 study out of the University of Toronto found that when individuals are in more anonymous settings, they can become even more forthcoming and helpful.[6] Other studies suggest that online environments can promote increased honesty, creativity, risk taking, and inclusivity. Basically, when we aren't being constantly evaluated, we

- Feel freer to take risks and share new ideas
- Less afraid of failing or looking foolish
- More honest about challenges and mistakes

 **Virtual Tip**

Give Kudos: Establish virtual boards where people can post anonymous compliments or words of encouragement.[7]

Autonomy Fuels Motivation

In addition to allowing employees to be better versions of themselves, remote work shifts the locus of control. Instead of working to please a manager (because now the manager can't *see* the daily choices being made), remote workers are asked to rely on their own decision-making skills and self-discipline. This subtle shift moves employee motivation from *external* compliance to *internal* commitment. Studies suggest that this type of autonomy has a much deeper impact on employee satisfaction and drive than external influences like the watchful gaze of a supervisor.[8] The best part is that internal motivation is more long-lasting than external motivation, which often disappears once the supervisor has left the room or logged out of the virtual office.

AMPLIFY COMMUNICATION

CLARIFY DIRECTION

BUILD PREDICTABILITY

REDEFINE ACCOUNTABILITY

CREATE CONNECTIONS

EQUIP YOUR PEOPLE

Another Personal Peggy Case Study: The Scowling Dean

Many years ago, I learned some valuable lessons about autonomy. Right out of college, I got a job as a middle school social studies teacher. I was excited as I organized my lesson plans and arranged my new classroom. It wasn't until the second day of class that I began to understand how little control I actually had. I was in the middle of a compelling lesson on the settlers making their way in the New World when the supervising dean, a large man with small glasses, slowly walked into the back of the room. He spent the rest of the class period standing there, arms folded across his chest, gazing over his tiny spectacles with a frown, watching as I managed the classroom. I felt myself start to sweat. After class, he let me know about the student in the back who was chewing gum and suggested I needed to get better control of the class. He came back often, making sure I was taking care of gum chewers and becoming the kind of teacher he expected me to be.

That experience shaped me for my entire short-lived middle school teaching career. I found myself stressed, never knowing when he would step in and correct me. I was afraid to try out new teaching ideas. I spent hours preparing lesson plans that I thought would make the dean happy. I felt trapped, watched, and incompetent, never able to totally trust myself or my teaching skills. At the end of that year, I turned in my resignation, convinced I was definitely *not* cut out for teaching.

The next year I picked up an adjunct teaching job at a nearby college. Surprisingly, I found no scowling administrator in the back of the room, no one waiting for me to make a mistake, no one telling me how to do my job. I had autonomy in this new role. I started testing new ideas, teaching in ways that fit my personality, and leveraging my humor and spontaneity. Sometimes I failed.

Sometimes I was amazing. It wasn't long before I fell in love with teaching—for real.

When we have the ability to make choices about our work, without the direct control and supervision of an external authority, we can discover a natural fit between our role and our strengths, finding unique ways to leverage what we do best.

Autonomy Fuels Productivity

Productivity studies are routinely used to better understand how the remote workplace impacts an organization's bottom line. While results are mixed, primarily due to the types of roles being studied, there are clear indications that remote and hybrid workers are significantly more productive than their in-person counterparts. An important study published by *Harvard Business Review* found a number of benefits when employees had more autonomy and felt empowered by their leaders. These employees

- Demonstrated increased creativity

- Were more committed to helping their colleagues

- Found more meaning in their jobs

- Felt more competent

- Put in additional effort to help their organization succeed

- Were more convinced that their work made a difference

- Experienced increased trust in their leaders[9]

It is clear that employee autonomy is one of the greatest opportunities to be found in the remote workplace. It enables individuals to flexibly create a work environment that suits their strengths and creates a space where employees feel trusted and empowered to do good work.

AMPLIFY COMMUNICATION

CLARIFY DIRECTION

BUILD PREDICTABILITY

REDEFINE ACCOUNTABILITY

CREATE CONNECTIONS

EQUIP YOUR PEOPLE

Accountability and Autonomy: It's a Balance

As positive as autonomy is, *full* employee autonomy can result in more problems than solutions. It can lead to inconsistencies, miscommunications, faulty assumptions, and frustration for both the leader and the employee.

The best leaders are able to find a balance. They create a culture of ownership, where employees feel trusted to manage their work but are also held responsible for results.

It really is all about balance—but the ideal balance of autonomy and accountability will be different for each situation. Let's take a look at some of the key determining factors.

The Role: How Much Autonomy Is Possible?

Clearly, not every role allows for complete flexibility. Some jobs—like those in call centers, manufacturing, healthcare, and security operations—require employees to be available at specific times or to follow strict procedures. But that doesn't mean autonomy is impossible. Even in highly structured roles, employees can be given some level of choice. This might take the form of flexible break schedules, or allowing employees to innovate within their scope or to adjust their task order or workflow based on personal efficiency.

Even small areas of autonomy can lead to greater engagement.

Case Study: A Call Center Autonomy Experiment

A financial services company had a rigidly structured call center where agents followed strict scripts and schedules. They felt it was important to control their message and wanted to make sure their employees were getting it right. Unfortunately, leadership noticed high rates of burnout and turnover.

AMPLIFY COMMUNICATION

CLARIFY DIRECTION

BUILD PREDICTABILITY

REDEFINE ACCOUNTABILITY

CREATE CONNECTIONS

EQUIP YOUR PEOPLE

So, they decided to experiment with giving more experienced employees the ability to customize call scripts to sound more natural. They also allowed team members to swap shifts without manager approval. As long as key metrics were met, employees were able to deal with customer calls in their own way.

The result?

- Customer satisfaction rose by 15 percent.

- Call times decreased by 9 percent.

- Turnover dropped by 22 percent, as employees felt increasingly trusted and valued.

 **Virtual Tip**

Provide choice: Find opportunities, even small ones, that will allow remote employees to make choices in how they do their work.

The Employee: Who's Ready for More Freedom?

Not all employees thrive with greater autonomy. We know that experience, personality, and motivation levels vary, so it's critical to tailor the amount of autonomy to the individual. For instance, new or less experienced employees may need more structure and guidance before they can handle a work mode with a high degree of autonomy. The key is to scale up in stages:

1. Start with structured guidance.

2. Monitor progress using clear metrics and goals.

3. Gradually let employees take ownership.

4. If they handle it well, increase their autonomy.

According to Tony Diekemper, a noted leadership consultant and experienced CEO, the ability to work more independently should be based on past performance: "Reliability earns flexibility . . . the more trustworthy the employee is, the more flexibility in scheduling they should earn."[10]

 **Virtual Tip**

Encourage a problem-solving mindset: Ask questions; don't give answers immediately. When employees (especially new or younger employees) come to you with problems, respond with open-ended questions that help them develop their self-sufficiency:

"What options have you considered so far?"

"What do you think is the best way forward?"

The Manager: Can YOU Let Go of Control?

Many managers struggle to embrace autonomy—not because they don't trust their teams, but because they grew up in organizations where micromanagement was the norm. Or maybe the skepticism is a result of getting burned in the past, feeling disrespected in the present, or being worried about the future. There are a lot of reasons it is hard to give up control, especially when we can't see our employees doing their jobs.

On a personal level, David will be the first to admit this is a struggle. Letting go hasn't been easy, but the trust and commitment we've seen as a result of increased employee autonomy has made it clear that the rewards far outweigh the initial discomfort.

Case Study: The Micromanaging CEO Who Nearly Lost His Team

A software startup had a CEO who couldn't let go of control. He tracked employee logins and activity every hour. In addition, he required daily reports on what each person accomplished.

AMPLIFY COMMUNICATION

CLARIFY DIRECTION

BUILD PREDICTABILITY

REDEFINE ACCOUNTABILITY

CREATE CONNECTIONS

EQUIP YOUR PEOPLE

He finally reached out to us for help after almost all of his top engineers quit, citing lack of trust and constant pressure. The CEO realized he had to make a shift in how he managed.

It didn't happen all at once, but changes were made:

- He stopped tracking hours and started focusing on results. These results were clear, measurable, and created through collaboration between division heads and their employees.

- He worked at trusting employees to own their projects—as long as they delivered.

- He scheduled weekly check-ins for alignment, but let employees manage the rest of their time.

From that point on, trust was built. He noticed significant increases in innovative problem solving. As he demonstrated trust in his employees, he felt less pressure to micromanage and was better able to focus on bigger, more strategic goals. Employee morale rebounded, and **turnover dropped by almost 40 percent**.

 ## Virtual Tip

Trust first, monitor second: If employees are delivering results, resist the urge to micromanage. Instead of tracking activity, track outcomes:

- Did they meet their deadlines?
- Is their quality of work high?
- Are they engaged in team discussions?

If performance slips, address it directly—but don't assume remote work leads to slacking off.

Accountability Benchmark Survey

Let's take a minute to see where your accountable autonomy balance currently lies.

1. **I believe my team members are capable of completing their work without diligent oversight.**

   1 = Are you kidding? As soon as I sign off, I'm pretty sure they quit working.

   5 = I fully trust that they are working just as hard, if not harder, when I am not watching them.

   1   2   3   4   5

2. **I encourage employees to make decisions independently within their roles.**

   1 = Sorry—if I am ultimately responsible, I will make the decisions.

   5 = I regularly find ways to give employees decision-making power.

   1   2   3   4   5

3. **Mark the place on this continuum where you tend to feel the most comfortable.**

   _____

   Hold employees accountable   Give employees autonomy

4. **I rely on outcome-based metrics (results, deliverables) rather than monitoring activity (hours logged, online status).**

   1 = It's hard for me to trust outcome-based supervising. It usually doesn't work.

   5 = I don't worry about how my employees spend their days, as long as they deliver results.

   1   2   3   4   5

5. We have developed clear expectations so I can more easily hold team members accountable.

1 = They have their job descriptions, but it's hard for me to know exactly what they should be doing.

5 = I have a shared understanding with each employee about what they are expected to be accomplishing.

1   2   3   4   5

6. I feel comfortable providing my team members consistent feedback, both positive and negative.

1 = I don't give much feedback. It feels so awkward.

5 = I have created a climate where we can easily discuss both the positives and the negatives of their work.

1   2   3   4   5

7. Which areas of accountability do you think your employees wish you were better at?

Applying Your Results

Questions 1, 2, and 3 are designed to help you think about where you are most comfortable and where you think the balance *should* be in your unique workplace.

Effective accountability in this model hinges on creating measurable outputs. Questions 4–7 are designed to help you start thinking about changes you may need to make to implement the full power of accountable autonomy.

Accountable Autonomy: Building an Accountability Culture *without Micromanaging*

Holding employees accountable in a remote setting requires a fundamental shift from **supervision-based management** to **results-driven leadership**. Employees don't need constant oversight—they need:

1. Transparent measurement of work

2. Clear expectations

3. Consistent feedback

4. Appropriate consequences

Let's take a look at what this requires.

Rethink Measurement: Focus on Results, Not Hours

Many remote leaders still struggle with not being able to "see" employees working. But time logged in is no longer a useful measure of productivity. **What matters is results.**

Jody Thompson, co-creator of Best Buy's pioneering flexible work model, sees this new type of remote accountability as a true shift in perspective: "This is a moment when working can change for the better. We need to create a different kind of work culture, where everyone is 100 percent accountable and 100 percent autonomous. **Just manage the work, not the people.**"[11]

✔ Virtual Tip

Improve transparency: Use project management tools that require clear metrics, milestones, and timelines. This kind of shared software will clarify expectations and give managers visibility into employee tasks without the need for micromanaging.

Clear Expectations

Here's something we can all agree on: We can't be held accountable for things we don't know we are responsible for. **Ambiguity is the enemy of accountability.** Clarity can provide direction and certainty for the remote employee, but it also allows the manager to more effectively measure and understand the progress being made.

Clarity is the key. For instance, instead of "You do the follow-up," try "Please create a three-page client report summarizing the meeting by Friday at 3 p.m. The report should include key decisions, action items, and client concerns."

Clarity means work can be measured, goals can be adjusted, and accomplishments can be celebrated.

 **Virtual Tip**

Use numbers: Include numbers in goals whenever possible. Clarify details like

- What date is it due?
- How many hours should be spent on this project?
- What is the target number of pages, sales, phone calls, etc.?

Trusted Leader Advice

Joe Kimbell, owner and president of World of Travel, has found one of the benefits of remote work to be that the entire organization is forced to be clearer about goals and expectations: "Now that we work remotely, I have evaluated our systems much more often than ever before, making sure we are all doing things consistently."[12]

Consistent Feedback

Once the foundation is laid, there needs to be regular accountability conversations that keep everyone working with the same understanding. Unfortunately, when most people think of accountability, they think of year-end reviews containing unexpectedly harsh criticism, or after-project debriefs that feel more like blame sessions than learning opportunities. No one looks forward to *that* kind of feedback.

On the other hand, helpful feedback can become a positive part of the everyday culture of an organization. Sometimes that includes an honest, hard-to-hear evaluation. Sometimes it includes authentic praise for projects (small or large) that have been done well. When these everyday conversations that include both positive and negative assessments happen on a regular basis, feedback becomes predictable and less anxiety-producing. It also helps employees see that one big mistake or critical comment doesn't mean the end of a promising career.

Unfortunately, most managers wait too long to give feedback to their employees. That is especially true in remote settings, where the "out of sight, out of mind" principle makes it easy to avoid difficult conversations. Remember:

- Frequent feedback prevents surprises.

- Feedback lets employees know where they stand.

- Early feedback keeps small problems from becoming big ones.

Never underestimate the power of compassionate and honest communication when it comes to developing trust. As a leader, consider how *you* can model healthy accountability by **asking for feedback on your own performance**.

 **Virtual Tip**

The "1-2-3" feedback framework: Want a simple way to structure feedback? Try this:

1. What's going well?

2. What needs improvement?

3. What's one action step moving forward?

This framework balances praise with constructive feedback, helping employees stay engaged while seeking out opportunities for improvement.

Appropriate Consequences: Address Poor Performance—Swiftly

Any experienced manager knows that written expectations and regular communication will not resolve all employee challenges, especially in the remote workplace. When productivity slips or expectations are not being met, **the accountable autonomy balance has to shift**. In these cases, it is even more important that transparency become part of the process. Those virtual stories woven in the silence of remote offices mean that if managers don't take the time to intentionally talk about the problem, employees won't get the message.

Here is one immutable truth: Nothing erodes team trust and morale faster than watching a coworker get away with bad behavior over and over again. This kind of impact is only amplified in the remote workplace. Thanks to the speed of digital communication, employees who see coworkers consistently miss deadlines, disappear from meetings, make disrespectful comments, and have a generally bad attitude—all with no real consequences—will share their grievances with everyone else in the organization faster than you can say the words "performance improvement plan." Waiting to see

AMPLIFY COMMUNICATION

CLARIFY DIRECTION

BUILD PREDICTABILITY

REDEFINE ACCOUNTABILITY

CREATE CONNECTIONS

EQUIP YOUR PEOPLE

if the drama goes away on its own is rarely a good strategy in a virtual environment. There are just too many assumptions, too much uncertainty, and too much isolation to let normal conflict, underperformance, and bad behavior simply "resolve itself."

 **Virtual Tip**

Be clear and kind: To keep accountability professional, productive, and fair, use the Clear and Kind Correction Model.

Wrong approach:

"You're not working hard enough.

"It doesn't seem like you care."

"You must be taking too many breaks during the day."

"You're not contributing to our team meetings."

Better approach:

Step 1: Describe the issue.
"I've noticed you've missed two deadlines in the past month."

Step 2: Express expectations.
"We need reports submitted on time to keep projects moving."

Step 3: Offer support.
"What's getting in the way of meeting deadlines? How can I help?"

Step 4: Set clear next steps.
"Let's check in next Friday to ensure we're back on track."

Final Thought: Trust, Measure, Adjust

Remote teams can be highly accountable—but it takes intentional effort:

- Set clear expectations.

- Measure results, not hours.

- Give frequent, honest feedback.

- Hold employees accountable when needed.

By embracing accountable autonomy, leaders can build high-performing, high-trust teams—no micromanagement required.

AMPLIFY COMMUNICATION

CLARIFY DIRECTION

BUILD PREDICTABILITY

REDEFINE ACCOUNTABILITY

CREATE CONNECTIONS

EQUIP YOUR PEOPLE

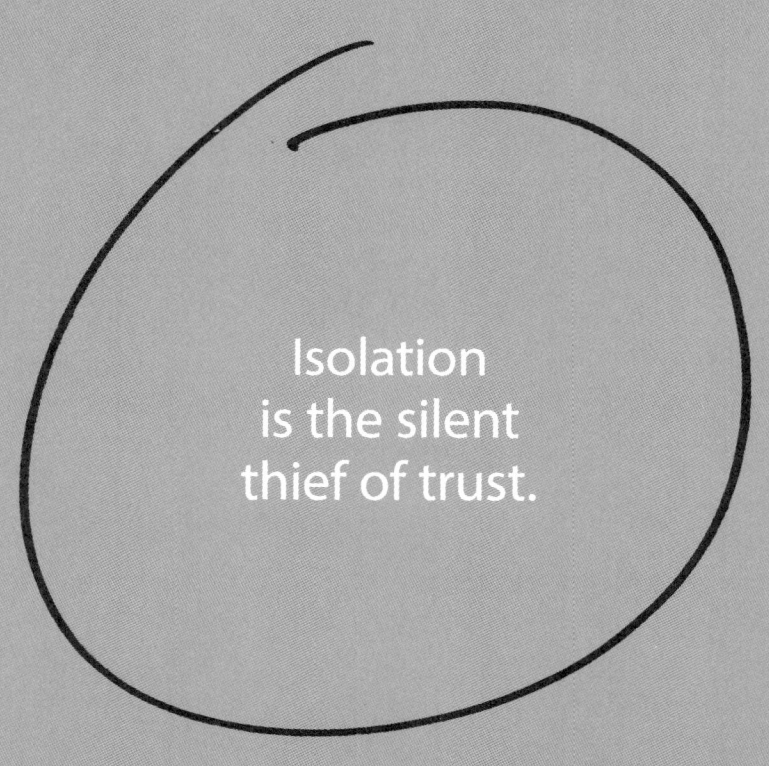

Isolation
is the silent
thief of trust.

CREATE CONNECTIONS

Bridge the distance through
a new kind of belongingness.

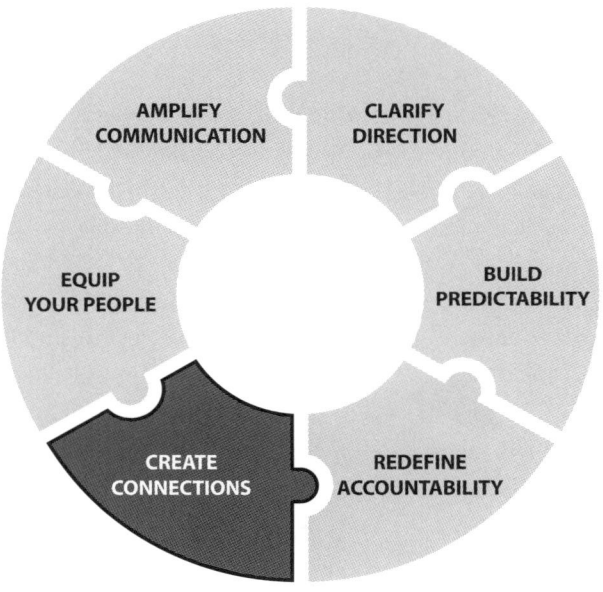

The remote workplace is full of potential, promising both free-dom and flexibility to create work environments that function better for everyone. But along with these benefits comes a hidden cost—one that can deeply impact personal well-being, motiva-tion, and trust.

So far, we've spent a lot of time focusing on strategies, logistics, and efficiency in remote work—but the relational challenges are just as significant, if not more so. Simply put: **People need people.**

Case Study: David's Faces of Sadness Video Call

At the height of the COVID-19 pandemic, I was leading a virtual training for a group of frontline nurses. These professionals were working an enormous number of hours in highly emotional, completely overwhelming circumstances.

As I began, I noticed very few participants had their cameras turned on and could sense that discussion was going to be nonexistent. It immediately became clear that my regular approach to facilitation was not going to work, not to mention that it would simply be inappropriate. I broke off my usual introduction and asked each of the nurses on the call to find a piece of paper and a pen and take a minute to draw what they were feeling at that exact moment. Then I asked them to turn on their cameras and hold up their drawings for all to see. What I saw took my breath away. There were hand-drawn faces of sadness, exhaustion, and anger. Many of the pages included words like *empty* and *broken*. We sat in silence, taking in what we were all experiencing together. In that moment, those nurses felt seen. And in that moment, we built trust.

This experience taught me a powerful lesson: People need to feel acknowledged and valued—especially in remote and hybrid workplaces. No matter how we organize it, remote work breeds isolation, isolation breeds loneliness, and loneliness erodes trust. This may be the biggest cost of all.

The Growing Epidemic of Isolation

Isolation is not just an issue for remote workers. As a culture, we are more isolated than ever before. It's easy to think it all started because of the pandemic, but the fact is, people in the United States were experiencing increased levels of isolation well before that.

According to the 2023 Surgeon General's report, between 2003 and 2020, the time an "average American" spent alone *increased* by over 24 hours per month, and the time spent with friends *decreased* by more than 20 hours per month.[1] This increased social isolation comes with a cost—the report notes that

- Lacking social connections can be "as dangerous as smoking up to 15 cigarettes a day."

- Pervasive feelings of loneliness can lead to high blood pressure, increased risk of stroke, heart attack, obesity, Alzheimer's disease, depression, and anxiety.[2]

Clearly, loneliness and social isolation are significant public health concerns—and the risk is compounded for those in remote offices. It's probably no surprise that a large-scale study out of Norway found that **one in four remote workers report feeling lonely "a lot of the day."**[3]

When these kinds of challenges are left unaddressed, our remote workers *will* **suffer**.

If we are going to build trust at a distance, we must be aware of the very real threats to well-being faced by our employees. We need to make sure we are protecting them from the natural dangers that exist in the virtual world.

Trusted Leader Advice

Debbie Gray, regional director with Behavioral Health Group, assigns one individual to focus just on remote leaders—especially those who are providing services in places that are literally remote. "That one person is able to take the extra time to pour into the remote supervisors. They use daily check-ins to answer questions and provide encouragement and support. The service providers really appreciate the extra connection."[4]

Connection Benchmark Survey

Let's take a minute to see where you're at with creating connections in your workplace.

1. **I give my full attention to video conversations, avoiding distractions like emails or my phone.**

   1 = I try, but I have *so much* going on!!

   5 = I concentrate fully on my employees during video calls, often muting notifications.

   1   2   3   4   5

2. **I pay attention to nonverbal cues (tone of voice, pacing, facial expressions) in video calls to better understand the speaker's emotions and attitudes.**

   1 = Sorry. If they can't say it, it must not be that important.

   5 = I regularly try to decipher my employees' feelings or intent by "reading between the lines."

   1   2   3   4   5

3. **Before I end remote conversations, I make sure we have a shared understanding.**

   1 = I have meetings scheduled back to back, so I usually just finish talking and I'm out.

   5 = I show respect to people in the meeting by making sure everyone's questions are answered and they know their next steps before we end.

   1   2   3   4   5

4. **I engage in social conversations with my team.**

1 = I don't like trying to be a boss *and* a friend. I'm pretty private.

5 = I frequently share parts of my non-work life with my employees.

1   2   3   4   5

5. **Our balance of work with team-building and social time seems appropriate.**

1 = We get down to business and that's about it.

5 = We usually spend way too much time chit-chatting in our meetings.

1   2   3   4   5

6. **Describe any "middle school" behaviors you think might be happening in your team (cliques, gossip, bullying).**

7. **If you were to ask your employees how connected you are to the team, what would they say?**

Applying Your Results

Questions 1, 2, and 3 are about whether you're *really* paying attention. If you're unsure, in your next few meetings, try specifically focusing on how you are coming across to your remote employees. Are you showing support, interest, and connection? Or do you communicate busyness, aloofness, and marginalization?

Questions 4–7 gauge how close your employees feel to you and to each other. If this is an area where you'd like to improve, don't worry! The next section is packed with practical ideas.

AMPLIFY COMMUNICATION

CLARIFY DIRECTION

BUILD PREDICTABILITY

REDEFINE ACCOUNTABILITY

CREATE CONNECTIONS

EQUIP YOUR PEOPLE

Creating Connections in Remote Work

A remote workplace can feel isolating if relationships aren't intentionally cultivated. But here's the good news: **Connection is possible—even at a distance.**

There are three key steps to building connection:

1. **Pay attention.** Show employees they are valued.

2. **Share.** Let people get to know the *real* you.

3. **Cultivate community.** Create spaces where belonging can thrive.

Let's take a look at each of these.

Pay Attention

One of the clearest threats to psychological safety and trust is when it seems like a manager just doesn't care enough to pay attention. There is a pervasive feeling that many remote managers are **too busy**.

This bears repeating, because it's something we hear *over and over*. Remote workers regularly feel that their managers are too busy for them. The interesting part of this finding is that most of these busy managers don't even realize what they are communicating or what kind of impact their distracted communication is having.

Busy leaders **inherently value** their employees but **unconsciously adopt** online behaviors that communicate just the opposite:

- They work on other tasks during video meetings.

- They frequently miss meetings or check-ins.

- They end meetings abruptly to get to the next (more important) meeting.

- They send incomplete or cryptic texts.

- They ghost employees by not returning emails or chat messages.

One of the most meaningful ways to build trust in the remote workplace is to simply pay attention—to how we communicate, how we show up in conversations, and how we make others feel heard. It sounds simple, but any remote manager knows how hard it is to be fully present.

Let's face it. We're busy. Our remote workspaces are often set up with multiple screens, each filled with separate projects and conversations, each demanding our too often divided attention. No wonder so many leaders look distracted in virtual meetings! But here's the real problem: In a remote setting, where misunderstandings and assumptions run wild, nothing destroys trust faster than the real or imagined perception of being ignored or marginalized by a boss.

Your employees notice when you're distracted. And if they feel unheard, no words of support will be enough to fix it. Instead, prioritize, focus, and start paying attention:

- **Commit.** Before you meet with a direct report, remind yourself: "It is my job to help them succeed."

- **Look at the person you are talking to.** Eye contact works. Sure, you may be looking at a screen and not *actually* looking in their eyes, but at least you aren't looking at something else.

- **Turn off notifications.** *Ding!* No matter how disciplined you are, an email or chat notification will distract you from the conversation you're having. Minimize email or anything else that will silently summon your attention.

- **Begin to notice what is *not* being said in the conversation.** Be curious about what's just below the surface of your employee's hesitancy or carefully chosen words.

- **Respond** with active listening techniques:

  - **Smile and nod.** People can tell when you're engaged—even virtually.

  - **Mirror emotions.** If they look frustrated, respond with concern. If they seem excited, join in the enthusiasm.

- **Clarify with questions** like, "Can you say more about that?"
- **Summarize what you heard** with comments like, "Okay, let me know if I got this right . . ."

It's amazing how a little more focus on active listening can help the person you are talking to feel seen, heard, and valued.

✔ Virtual Tip

Summarize: Strengthen your team's listening habits by asking each team member to summarize the previous speaker's ideas before moving on to the thought they want to add. This ensures members **listen actively** instead of simply waiting for their turn to talk.

Share

In addition to showing people you are paying attention (and then actually paying attention), **modeling authenticity** can create important social bonds that increase psychological safety and trust. That doesn't mean oversharing, but it does mean letting people see a little bit of the *real* you:

- Had a great weekend with your kids? Share a quick story.

- Moving an aging parent into assisted living? Share some of your journey. You may find out there are other team members on the same road.

- Feel like your presentation wasn't great? Own it, then talk about how you'll improve next time.

- Next time someone asks, "How are you?" **actually tell them.**[5]

✔ Virtual Tip

Admit mistakes: Demonstrating humility and honesty encourages employees to openly share their own failures and concerns with you and with each other.

People may admire your wins, but they can connect with your struggles. When employees see their leader as a real person who learns, struggles, and grows, it creates a foundation of trust and connection—one that will benefit the entire team.

How much should you reveal? Not everyone is comfortable socializing with people they don't know well or opening up about the more private elements of their life with employees.

Before stepping out and disclosing something personal, consider the following:

- **Time and place:** Is this the right moment to share? A casual team check-in? Share. A high-stakes client meeting? Keep it to yourself.

- **Relationship status:** The depth of disclosure should match the relationship. Sharing frustrations with a long-time colleague? That makes sense. With a new hire? Maybe hold back.

- **Comfort:** Some leaders *love* sharing. Others don't. If you're hesitant, start small. Maybe mention a favorite TV show or hobby before diving deeper.

- **Mistakes:** Being vulnerable is powerful—but balance is key. If you're in a leadership role, avoid disclosures that might undermine confidence in your decision making.

- **Motivation:** Consider *why* you are sharing something personal. Is it to create a safe space for your team so they feel comfortable sharing? Is it to help your team see you as a real person? Great. If you are sharing because you want people to like you or because you have no one else to help you process your feelings, then reconsider.

Even small glimpses into your life can help employees feel more comfortable, valued, and connected.

AMPLIFY COMMUNICATION

CLARIFY DIRECTION

BUILD PREDICTABILITY

REDEFINE ACCOUNTABILITY

CREATE CONNECTIONS

EQUIP YOUR PEOPLE

Cultivate Community

There is nothing more empowering and life-giving than feeling like a valued member of a team. That sense of belongingness can motivate and heal like few other things can. Team cohesiveness, complete with strong social bonds and high levels of trust, is what makes the remote workplace work.

Keep in mind, a **sense of community** is about more than just getting along—it's about feeling valued, seen, and supported. Research shows that strong workplace communities share these four traits:

1. Effective communication

2. High trust

3. Concern for each member's welfare

4. A shared sense of purpose[7]

In a recent survey of nearly 1,500 women, author and scholar Christine Porath found that when workers felt a sense of community at work, they were more likely to thrive, experienced less stress, were more engaged, and were *far* more likely to stay with their current employer.[8] In many ways, a strong workplace community can provide the kind of well-being protection that remote workers are looking for.

Why Remote Work Makes Community Harder

Traditional offices can naturally foster connections. Employees bump into each other in hallways, chat over lunch, and share laughs between meetings. These unplanned interactions help form relationships and build trust.

Remote work, however, is different. Most virtual meetings are highly structured and transactional. People log in, cover their agenda items, and log off. Not much small talk. Not many laughs. Rare spontaneous connections. Without effort, working relationships in these contexts will slowly fade. The challenge for the remote manager is to facilitate interactions similar to those that happen naturally in the in-person office.

Helping a team connect, both socially and emotionally, isn't easy. It can be tricky to find the right balance between creating opportunities that are structured but not too forced, rewarding but not too time-consuming, and creative but not too cheesy. Here are a few ideas to get you started:

- **Socialize.** To build community in remote teams, "infuse opportunities for friendship into meetings."[9] A little social time goes a long way. Instead of making employees choose between productivity and connection, build quick, natural moments of interaction into existing meetings:
  - Dedicate the first five minutes of staff meetings to casual conversation.
  - Before meetings start, invite employees to share a quick non-work highlight from their week.
  - Use breakout rooms for informal chats before meetings begin, after they end, or during times of discussion or brainstorming.

- **Have fun.** Even if not every team member is a lover of celebrations that include silly hats and goofy games, there is value

AMPLIFY COMMUNICATION

CLARIFY DIRECTION

BUILD PREDICTABILITY

REDEFINE ACCOUNTABILITY

CREATE CONNECTIONS

EQUIP YOUR PEOPLE

in finding experiences that help the team laugh together. Research consistently shows that these kinds of group memories and inside jokes strengthen cohesiveness.[10] It is those shared experiences that serve to remind each team member they are part of something special. Think about how you might add a little fun to your team's workweek—for example:

- Schedule a shared lunch hour so people in the same time zone can chat while eating lunch.

- Create mid-afternoon shared coffee breaks.

- Take connected group walks around the block.

- Begin a ritual where everyone shares something good that happened in the team chat at the end of the day.

- Open a specific messaging channel just for exchanging jokes or words of encouragement.

- Have a regular game time where whoever is available plays an online game every Friday after work.

- End Friday wrap-up meetings with a trivia session, where the trivia is related to the history or mission of the company.

- Persuade employees to come into the office one day a week by providing a complimentary lunch for everyone.

- **Be strategic.** Formal, facilitated team-building exercises can also help build community. These kinds of strategic experiences help teams identify challenges and leverage opportunities as they do their work together. They include

  - **In-person retreats** where strategic planning and goal setting are mixed with social experiences and fun

  - **Workshops** that help team members understand communication styles, strengths, and challenges

  - **Assessments** like DiSC[11] or CliftonStrengths,[12] to help employees better understand themselves and each other

- **Acknowledge the team.** The way we provide recognition and rewards communicates a lot about what we value. If building strong, cohesive teams is a priority, consider the reward system. Goals that are individual and competitive in nature encourage doing what it takes to be better than others on the team. You may end up with a winner, but that means you have a whole group of losers. If your goal is to build a feeling of community, shift to team-based rewards:

    - Recognize team achievements publicly.

    - Offer group incentives (lunches, bonuses, time off).

    - Celebrate collective wins over individual milestones.

✔ Virtual Tip

Highlight the team: Publicly acknowledge the team's good work (not just individual efforts), especially when communicating with senior leadership or important external stakeholders. Make sure to use pronouns like "we" and "us" instead of "I" and "you."

The Balance between Connection and Productivity

Providing space for fun and socialization can actually be a challenging proposition. Too much time socializing may begin to feel repetitive, inauthentic, and a waste of time. However, not enough socializing will have a direct impact on the team's ability to navigate difficult situations, including deadlines, failures, conflicts, and inefficiencies, simply because team members haven't built enough trust. Developing remote connections can take time, but the trust that is developed will have a direct impact on productivity and satisfaction.

Case Study: Peggy's Distrusting Team

A team of young leaders was tasked with giving regular project presentations to the executive leaders. Each member of the team was smart, kind, easy to get along with, and naturally good at presenting. But when they presented their first formal progress report, I was horrified by how poorly they did. There was repeated information, opposing information, missing information, and a lack of big-picture information. The worst thing? They looked absolutely miserable. The team members were frustrated with themselves and with each other, and it showed.

After the presentation, we met together in a videoconference to talk about what had happened. The problem? They didn't trust each other. These high achievers were each so focused on their individual performance that they weren't willing to rely on one another; they didn't trust their team members to get it right.

Over several weeks, we spent time getting to know one another. We used a DiSC assessment to talk about each of their strengths and differences, and we slowly created a safe space for each person to share some of their misunderstandings and frustrations. We even played an online escape room. (Okay. It wasn't as painful as I expected.) It was when we finally escaped from that virtual room that I saw the team members start to smile and crack jokes. The whole thing took time—more time than I had planned for—but it worked. Their final presentation flowed like clockwork, and they seemed to actually enjoy themselves.

Building trust takes time, but when employees feel like they belong to a team, they work better together. Belonging is especially important as we seek to protect our remote employees. A mutual feeling of camaraderie can help remote workers feel a little less remote, a little less lonely, and a little better connected.

Beware the Dark Side

Building a strong sense of community is an important way to protect your people from the isolation and mental health challenges lurking behind every virtual corner. As important as this is, however, we need to highlight something that gets far less attention: Sometimes we need to protect our people from each other.

Psychology and communication scholars have identified some of the shadowy behaviors that can happen in online groups. According to the social identity deindividuation effects model (SIDE),[13] when an online group becomes highly cohesive, members can lose their personal set of moral guidelines, and the group as a whole will start to disregard social expectations, acting out in ways that can be damaging to the entire organization.

For instance, groups may devolve into gossiping about others and negatively stereotyping non-group members. Harsh insider/outsider dynamics are created where coworkers are excluded, made fun of, or bullied. Unfortunately, damage caused by the group's behavior is all too often minimized or ignored.

Certainly, social tension can arise in any workplace, whether remote or in-person—but the anonymity of the virtual world makes these challenges even more dangerous. The inherent disconnection from a physical reality creates an environment where individuals can act **without seeing the harm they are inflicting** on others, and where they are **rarely held accountable** for the pain they cause.

 Virtual Tip

Honor the absent: Encourage team members to be mindful of stereotypes, especially related to people from other teams. Adopt a practice of only speaking good about someone when they aren't present.

It's almost offensive to advise remote managers to watch out for and address problems with cliques and bullies—after all, we are responsible, mature adults. But we have seen these negative group behaviors cause more harm than you'd ever imagine. To build trust

AMPLIFY COMMUNICATION

CLARIFY DIRECTION

BUILD PREDICTABILITY

REDEFINE ACCOUNTABILITY

CREATE CONNECTIONS

EQUIP YOUR PEOPLE

at a distance, remote managers need to be aware of the power of groups, both to do good and to inflict harm.

It is up to the trusted leader to identify and break down social barriers. Here is some advice from leaders who have suffered through and overcome the dark side of remote social conflict:

- **Pay attention.** Listen to how employees inside a group talk about those outside the group. If certain employees never seem to be included in discussions, take action.

- **Mix it up.** Encourage cross-department collaboration, mentorship programs, and structured social interactions that integrate different teams.

- **Confront it.** Address workplace drama head-on: "Mark, I heard you were voicing some strong frustration about Tim at lunch. Let's talk about it privately—I want to make sure we're all on the same page."

- **Ask yourself:** *Do I tend to engage in the same stereotyping as everyone else on my team? Is it easy to blame certain people or make fun of them when they aren't present?*

A connected team is a stronger team—but only if that connection is positive and inclusive.

Trusted Leader Advice

According to Tony Diekemper, CEO and leadership expert, "If you have employee problems that you are not dealing with, being remote will just make them worse. You have to put energy into paying attention and wanting to find and solve those interpersonal conflicts."[14]

The Challenge of Work-Life Boundaries

In addition to protecting our employees from each other, we need to find ways to protect them from themselves. In many ways, the old-fashioned in-person boundaries between work life and home life helped us manage the competing demands of each. After all, we're different people at home and at work. When we're at work, we assume a professional role—administrator, supervisor, director—and behave and communicate in a way that is consistent with that role. When we're at home, we take on a different set of roles—spouse, parent, friend—and behave and communicate accordingly. Here's one thing we've learned: Our children don't appreciate being managed, and our employees don't tolerate being parented. Those roles don't easily overlap— or at least, they didn't use to.

During the pandemic, we were introduced to the challenge of doing **everything all at once, all in the same space**. We watched as colleagues cared for children, cooked dinner, and tried to deal with unruly pets, all while leading meetings or working with their teams. In a remote work environment, the boundaries that once made it easier for us to manage the different parts of our lives have faded, leaving remote workers susceptible to being **always on** and **always exhausted**:

- According to a 2022 study by Bloomberg, remote employees work on average three more hours per week than their in-office counterparts.[15]

- Nearly one-third of remote workers report that unplugging after work is their top challenge.[16]

- The inability to "turn off" work leads to higher levels of fatigue, stress, and burnout.[17]

Confronting the Threat

As leaders, it is important that we see the threat posed by the intense nature of the remote workplace and take action to mitigate its impact. There are steps we can take to help our remote employees reestablish some of the protections and natural boundaries they used to enjoy when part of an in-person office. Here are some suggestions:

- **Set clear expectations about work hours.** Create a culture where it's okay to be unavailable after a certain time. When possible, encourage employees to define their own "off-the-clock" hours and communicate them to the team.

- **Designate no-meeting days.** Dedicate certain days (or half-days) to focused work, free from meetings. This protects deep work time and helps prevent after-hours work catch-up sessions.

- **Implement a daily "power hour."** Block out an hour each day where employees are considered unavailable for messages or calls, allowing them to focus on their most important tasks.

- **Encourage physical and mental separation.** If possible, employees should create a dedicated workspace at home and implement end-of-day rituals—like shutting their laptops, tidying up, or writing tomorrow's to-do list—to symbolically signal that the workday is done.

- **Use Difference-Making Actions (DMAs).** Every morning, write down the **top three priorities** for the day—then check on them at the end of the day. This keeps employees focused on what truly matters, preventing work from creeping into personal time.

✔ Virtual Tip

Model healthy boundaries: Try not to send emails and messages after regular work hours. If it can wait, use "schedule send" or send it first thing the following day. Employees notice time-stamps and quickly internalize expectations based on what you are modeling.

Final Thought: A Connected Team Is a Trusting Team

Your role as a leader isn't just about getting work done—it's about creating an environment where people can thrive. In remote work, it requires conscious effort to build relationships, set boundaries, and create an inclusive culture. Trust grows when employees feel seen, heard, and protected.

AMPLIFY COMMUNICATION

CLARIFY DIRECTION

BUILD PREDICTABILITY

REDEFINE ACCOUNTABILITY

CREATE CONNECTIONS

EQUIP YOUR PEOPLE

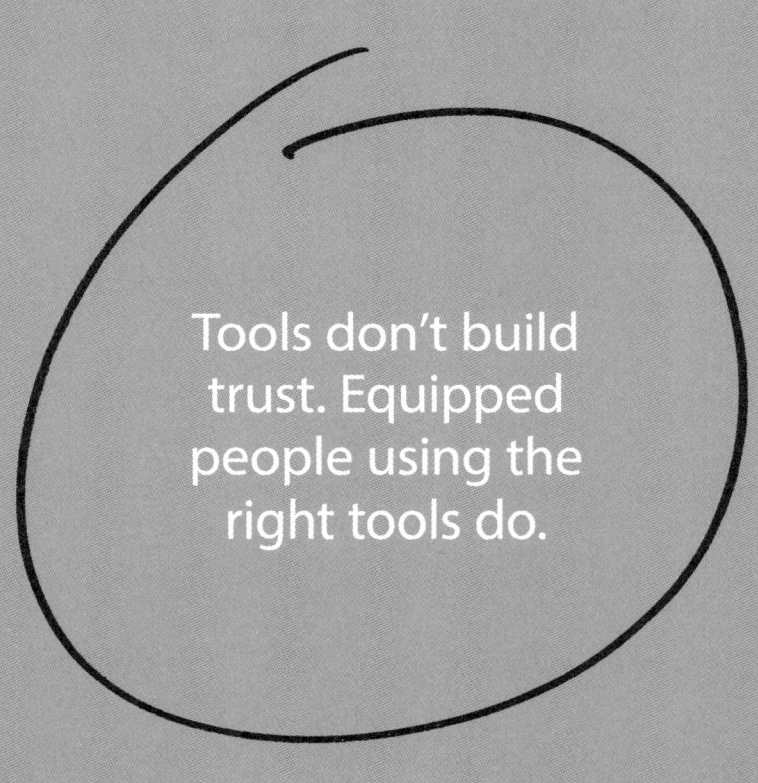

Tools don't build trust. Equipped people using the right tools do.

EQUIP YOUR PEOPLE

Intentionally train, develop, and update.
Don't let remoteness impact excellence.

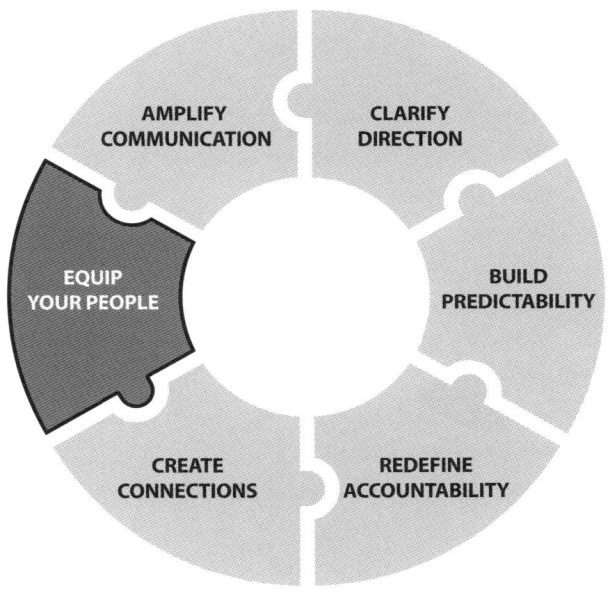

Genuinely empowering your team goes far beyond the routine of updating laptops every few years. While providing cutting-edge tools and essential equipment lays the groundwork for productivity, the true competitive edge comes from investing in your people—their development, growth, and potential. It's a powerful way to show that they are seen and supported, freeing them to focus on doing their best work.

Case Study: The High Cost of "Good Enough"

A large tech company that had recently shifted to a hybrid model hired a promising new software developer, Jake. On paper, Jake was perfect—great technical skills, a strong portfolio, and a solid interview. But within a few months, his manager noticed something wasn't quite right.

Jake's work was . . . **okay**. It wasn't bad, but it also wasn't great. He hit his deadlines, but he rarely took initiative. His code worked, but it wasn't efficient. He attended meetings, but he rarely spoke up.

Concerned, his manager scheduled a one-on-one. "Jake, how's everything going?" he asked.

Jake hesitated. "Honestly? I feel like I'm doing okay . . . but I don't really know what *great* looks like in this company."

That was the lightbulb moment.

Jake wasn't lazy or disengaged—he was underequipped. Working remotely meant that he wasn't exposed to the kinds of informal learning opportunities that arise in an office. He wasn't overhearing problem-solving discussions, watching senior developers work through challenges, or getting quick, in-the-moment feedback.

No wonder his work felt average. **He wasn't set up to do better.**

Competence is one of the most foundational aspects of trust. Jake's experience highlights a hidden challenge of remote work—the absence of natural learning opportunities. **Employees don't know what they don't know.** And without intentional effort from leadership, remote workers may settle for "good enough" instead of great.

Providing the Necessary Support

The trusted leader's role is to equip, encourage, and elevate. In the remote workplace, that includes providing support in three important areas:

- **Training** to build skills for the future

- **Career development** to foster long-term growth

- **Tools** to get their work done efficiently

When employees feel well equipped, they feel confident. When employees feel confident, they perform at their best. When employees perform at their best, trust grows. Let's take a look at how leaders can ensure their teams have the support they need to meet these goals.

Training

Ensuring that employees have the knowledge and skills necessary to be competitive in today's marketplace is key to building a competent workforce.

Case Study: The Fumbling Technology

A marketing agency recently moved to a hybrid work model. The organization prided itself on innovation, yet within months of going remote, leadership faced a problem they hadn't anticipated: Employees were struggling to keep up with the new technology, and it was impacting productivity.

One department, in particular, stood out. A seasoned manager, Maria, was leading a team that had always performed well in the office—but once they moved to a virtual setting, things started to unravel. Deadlines were missed, communication slowed, and frustration mounted. At first, Maria assumed the issue was motivation, but the real culprit was a **lack of training**. Her team had never been properly taught how to use the new tools—particularly the project management software. Without the informal learning that naturally happens in an office, they were left fumbling on their own.

The solution? A structured training program specifically designed for remote collaboration. Over the next several months, the company rolled out:

- Hands-on workshops
- Peer mentoring
- Easy-to-access video tutorials and reference guides

AMPLIFY COMMUNICATION

CLARIFY DIRECTION

BUILD PREDICTABILITY

REDEFINE ACCOUNTABILITY

CREATE CONNECTIONS

EQUIP YOUR PEOPLE

- In-person, cohort-based training

The impact was immediate: Efficiency increased, communication improved, and the employees' stress levels dropped significantly. Maria herself admitted that she had been hesitant about the changes, but that once she'd learned how to use the tools properly, she found they actually made her job easier.

This story highlights a critical truth: Just because employees are highly skilled in their jobs doesn't mean they are equipped to work remotely. If we want remote teams to thrive, we must be intentional about providing them with the training they need. This includes

- Technology skills
- Compliance and security protocols
- Leadership skills

Mastering Technology

Technology is evolving at an unprecedented pace. While all workplaces must adapt to new tools and platforms, remote employees are especially dependent on digital solutions for communication, collaboration, and productivity.

Today, being comfortable with technology isn't just an advantage—**it's a necessity**. If remote workers can't confidently navigate videoconferencing software, project management platforms, or team messaging apps, they will struggle to collaborate effectively.

 **Virtual Tip**

Conduct a skills-gap analysis: Ask employees which skills or tools they struggle with and what kind of training would help them work better or more efficiently.

Securing Compliance

One of the biggest blind spots in remote work is cybersecurity. Many companies invest in state-of-the-art security systems but forget that the greatest vulnerability is often human error. Employees who access sensitive company data through unsecured home WiFi networks or coffee shop hotspots can put the entire organization at risk.

As cybersecurity threats become more sophisticated, remote employees need to be trained on how to protect company information. We can't assume they're aware of and fully understand all the potential risks to organizational security.

Virtual Tip

Avoid unsecured channels for sensitive discussions: Remind employees not to discuss sensitive company information via unsecured platforms like text messaging or over the phone in public spaces. Reinforce best practices that pertain to your industry, such as using a VPN, keeping antivirus tools updated, and keeping all passwords secure.

Supporting the Softer Side

Keep in mind that technology isn't the only challenge remote employees face. **Time management, self-discipline, and virtual communication skills** are equally critical for success in a remote setting.

Some employees are naturally suited for remote work—they are self-starters, excellent at organizing their workload, and proactive in seeking feedback. Others struggle without the structure of an office environment. They may feel isolated, unsure of how to manage their time effectively, or hesitant to reach out for support.

Unfortunately, many leaders are promoted for their expertise, not necessarily for their ability to manage people—especially at a distance. Traditional leadership skills don't always translate well in a virtual setting, and without proper guidance, remote managers may unintentionally neglect key areas like communication, accountability, and connection.

 Virtual Tip

Offer training tailored to remote managers: Leadership in a virtual world is different, and it can be hard. Provide managers with tools and coaching to help them successfully navigate remote leadership.

Learning on the Fly

One of the biggest challenges in remote work is the **lack of real-time, on-the-job learning**. In a traditional office, new employees pick up skills by watching colleagues and asking quick questions. But in a remote setting, this kind of informal learning is much more difficult.

Think about a new hire joining a remote team. They might receive a few onboarding documents and maybe have a virtual welcome meeting, but after that, they're often left to figure things out on their own. In an office, they could observe how their teammates handle projects, or ask someone who looks nice and doesn't seem too busy to give them a bit of help if they get stuck. Online, they don't have that luxury. Without structured training and an ability to ask questions in real time, they will struggle to get up to speed.

Because **immediate feedback is essential** for skill development, companies should consider incorporating specific training approaches, such as

- Live training sessions
- Interactive simulations
- Structured onboarding mentorship programs

Training has always been a key aspect of helping a workforce gain, keep, and grow their competency. It's more important than ever to provide this kind of support for workers who are operating in an environment where missing information and isolation are everyday challenges. Remote work can't mean "figure it out on your own." It requires a much more proactive approach to learning.

Career Development

In today's remote and hybrid work environments, career development can feel elusive. Without the daily hallway conversations and impromptu mentoring moments, employees have trouble envisioning their career trajectory. What's at stake isn't just engagement—it's retention.

Case Study: The Forgotten Career

A young marketing specialist named Raj was bright, driven, and full of fresh ideas. When his company transitioned to a remote-first model, he was excited about the flexibility—no long commute, more control over his schedule, and fewer office distractions. But after a year, something unexpected happened.

Despite his hard work, Raj started to feel like his career had stalled. He watched as colleagues who spent more time in the office got promoted, received special assignments, and built relationships with senior leaders. Raj decided he had to become better known in the organization, so he reluctantly packed up his computer and moved back to the office.

Raj's experience is not unique. A 2023 survey of over 500 executives found that *62 percent of leaders* considered in-office time an important or very important factor in promotions and salary increases.[1] While few leaders deliberately favor in-person employees, the reality is that **visibility matters** in career growth. Remote employees—particularly those earlier in their careers—risk becoming virtually invisible.

This challenge creates a **trust issue.** Employees who feel overlooked, undervalued, or stuck in their roles will start to disengage. They may wonder if leadership truly has their best interests in mind, or if they need to leave the company to advance. And without intervention, many will do just that.

A simple truth underlies this observation: We are all more likely to stay committed to organizations where we see a clear path for growth.

The key to retaining and developing remote employees is helping them build social capital. Social capital—the network of relationships that provide access to opportunities, knowledge, and career advancement—plays a crucial role in who gets noticed, who gets mentored, and, ultimately, who gets promoted.

Leaders must be intentional about creating career growth opportunities for remote employees.

The Power of Mentorship

If you've ever had a mentor who helped shape your career, you know the difference it makes. A mentor can offer insights, encouragement, and strategic guidance that employees might not receive otherwise. Yet, despite its importance, mentorship is in short supply.

A recent study found that while 83 percent of younger workers view mentorship as crucial for their career, only 52 percent actually have a mentor.[2] The gap is even greater for remote employees, who have fewer organic opportunities to build these relationships.

A company we recently consulted for recognized this gap and launched a *Remote Rising Leaders* initiative. Each new remote hire was paired with a senior mentor outside their immediate team. These mentors provided not only career advice but also insider knowledge about the company: who to connect with, how to navigate challenges, and what opportunities to look for. The organization experienced a **30 percent increase in promotions for remote team members within a year.**

 **Virtual Tip**

Create structured mentorship opportunities: Assign remote employees a mentor who can guide them in skill development, networking, and career planning.

Expanding Social Capital for Remote Employees

Remote employees don't have the luxury of bumping into executives in the hallway. Without **visibility, advocacy, and relationships**, it's easy to get overlooked.

Here are four ways leaders can help remote employees expand their social capital and career opportunities:

1. Create meaningful connections.

Encourage **cross-departmental interactions** to expand professional networks. The more people remote employees interact with, the more opportunities they will have to build valuable relationships. Here are a few ways to put this into practice:

- Host informal virtual networking events where employees from different departments can connect.

- Encourage remote employees to schedule virtual coffee chats with colleagues in other areas of the company.

- Pair remote employees with in-office counterparts to ensure they stay informed on key discussions.

2. Share the spotlight.

Remote employees often get left in the background during meetings. **Give them high-visibility opportunities** that showcase their contributions. For example:

- Assign them leadership roles in client meetings or team projects.

- Encourage them to present updates to senior leadership.

- Nominate them for company awards or public recognition.

The more visible remote employees are, the more likely they are to be considered for promotions and leadership opportunities.

3. Amplify remote voices.

When hybrid teams meet, in-office employees **naturally dominate** the conversation. Virtual participants may struggle to get a word in, especially when side conversations happen in the room away from the microphone. As a leader, it's your job to make sure remote employees are heard. Here are some suggestions:

- Pause discussions to check in with remote team members. ("Before we move on, I want to get Sarah's thoughts on this.")
- Rotate facilitation roles. Let remote employees lead discussions or summarize key takeaways.
- Encourage remote employees to keep their cameras on—seeing faces builds engagement and credibility.

  Small shifts in meeting dynamics can ensure **all voices are valued**, regardless of location.

4. Develop strong mentorship and sponsorship programs.

Mentorship focuses on career guidance and professional development. Sponsorship takes it a step further—sponsors actively advocate for employees, helping them get promotions, key projects, and leadership roles. Organizations that prioritize both mentorship and sponsorship create more inclusive career advancement opportunities. Try these tips:

- Encourage senior leaders to mentor remote employees to provide career guidance.
- Assign remote employees a sponsor who will advocate for them in promotion discussions.
- Make mentorship programs formal to ensure equal access for both remote and in-office employees.

Remote employees want to know they have a future in your company. They want to see a **clear career path** that doesn't require them to be in the office five days a week just to stay competitive. Leaders who actively invest in the career growth of remote workers send a powerful message: *Your contributions matter. Your career matters. We see you, we value you, and we want you to succeed.*

That message builds **trust, loyalty, and long-term commitment**. By helping remote employees expand their social capital, gain visibility, and develop strong mentorship connections, organizations not only retain top talent but also cultivate the next generation of leaders—no matter where they are located.

Tools

The remote workplace could not exist if it were not for the many technological tools that make it possible to communicate, collaborate, share information, and keep track of projects. But **tools alone don't build trust**.

Neil Postman, one of the foundational scholars in the field of media ecology, made a wise observation about the always changing, always improving, always exciting technological tools that provide the foundation for remote work: "Technological change is a trade-off . . . a Faustian bargain. Technology giveth and technology taketh away. This means that for every advantage a new technology offers, there is always a corresponding disadvantage."[3] It would be short-sighted to recommend that workers adopt every shiny new tool that comes along without consideration of how these tools may impact the workplace and, ultimately, how they impact trust.

Project Management Software: Clarity or Clutter?

There is nothing more beautiful than a perfectly aligned Gantt chart—the colors, the assignments, the deadlines. The remote workplace is certainly easier to navigate when everyone can track what each team member is doing. It allows managers to clearly assign tasks and oversee the progression of a project. It allows remote workers to easily see how their work fits in with the whole and understand where holdups and barriers might ultimately impact their progress. A good project management tool will eliminate the need for employees to dig through piles of emails and internal messaging texts to find the information they need. Clarity and connection.

But, as with any piece of software, there is a downside. Online project management programs can drain precious time and resources. Here are just a few of the potential challenges:

- **Notification fatigue:** If employees receive too many alerts— task updates, deadline reminders, new assignments—it can disrupt deep work and create unnecessary stress.

- **Overcomplication:** Sometimes managing the platform takes more time than doing the work itself. Teams that spend more time updating project statuses than completing projects are using the wrong tool.

- **Loss of personal connection:** When all communication is reduced to checkboxes and status updates, employees may feel like cogs in a system rather than valued contributors.

Here are a few criteria to keep in mind when using shared project management tools in remote and hybrid teams:

- **Choose:** Make sure the tool is designed for the work you do. If it's too complicated or too simple, it will only serve to make employees frustrated.

- **Adapt:** Regularly assess the benefits and costs of using the tool, knowing that as your employees and their projects change, the software might need to change too. Make sure the tool is adapting to meet the needs of the people who use it and not the other way around.

- **Enhance trust:** Confirm the tool is not causing barriers related to clarity, predictability, autonomy, accountability, and connection. Consider how to adapt your internal process to make sure the information provided is clear and predictable, and relationships are leveraged and valued.

Videoconferencing: Connection or Exhaustion?

A Quick Peggy Memory: I clearly remember the first time I had a videoconference during the pandemic in 2020. Like many of you, my main personal stressors were washing my produce and wondering when the stores would restock toilet paper. Even before we started using videoconferencing for work, one of my friends organized a virtual "happy hour." Yes, it took almost a full half-hour to get everyone connected with their cameras and sound on, and yes, the happy hour was more like a happy ten minutes. Even so, I sensed the power of that little camera. It helped me feel less isolated and more connected than I had in weeks. Online videoconferencing software is truly an amazing gift. Without it, remote work would be isolating and difficult. But it does come with costs . . .

Video Fatigue

Sitting in back-to-back video meetings is so much more exhausting than back-to-back in-person meetings. By the end of the day, most of us are completely wiped out.

We hear this from a lot of people—and they're right. A study out of Stanford suggests a number of reasons why "Zoom fatigue" is actually something to consider.[4] According to the lead researcher, Jeremy Bailenson, videoconferencing introduces various unexpected cognitive pressures, including:

- **Sustained eye contact:** Eye contact—even virtual eye contact—requires an unexpected amount of emotional energy. In an in-person setting, we rarely look someone in the eye during the entire meeting. It's simply draining.

- **Personal focus:** When we watch ourselves as we speak, we're constantly making all sorts of micro assessments and adjustments. Sometimes it takes a lot of work to look so good! That kind of effort takes an enormous amount of cognitive energy.

- **Restricted movement:** Keeping in camera view automatically reduces our mobility. We often forget about taking quick breaks or walks around the room when we have one virtual meeting stacked up after another.

- **Filling in blanks:** We carry a heavier cognitive load going into a videoconference because we have to make so many assumptions, especially when we have such limited nonverbal information. We're constantly filling in the missing pieces. That takes even more energy.

- **Pixelated reality:** Looking at a screen is actually quite different from looking at something in real life. It's easy to forget that a video screen is made up of thousands of little pixels, each shining their very own little beam of light. Our brain smoothly forms these beams of lights into pictures that make sense—a cognitive process that also takes energy.

Try these five tips to reduce video fatigue:

1. **Reduce virtual eye contact.** Consider making your video screen small so the eye contact isn't quite so direct and intense.

2. **Choose the "hide self" view.** *This suggestion has been a personal game-changer* for Peggy. After a colleague suggested I hide the self-view box, my inevitable end-of-day headaches immediately began to disappear. As fun as it is to watch myself perform, it is truly exhausting.

3. **Move.** Walking around during a meeting might not be as questionable as you think.

4. **Make meetings interactive.** Use breakout rooms, polling, and screen sharing to keep engagement high.

5. **Schedule breaks.** Stop scheduling so many meetings, one on top of another! First of all, we probably don't need to meet

AMPLIFY COMMUNICATION

CLARIFY DIRECTION

BUILD PREDICTABILITY

REDEFINE ACCOUNTABILITY

CREATE CONNECTIONS

EQUIP YOUR PEOPLE

as often as we do. If an email or a text could suffice, use that instead. Second, always give yourself a few minutes between meetings. Seriously. *Give yourself a break!*

 Virtual Tip

Try standing: When you're presenting over video, or even when you feel yourself getting bored, stand up! That's it. Stand. It will add some of that energy that may get lost by talking to a screen.

Intra-Office Chat Channels: Communication or Chaos?

Another Peggy memory: when I first started using the intra-office chat, I thought it was the best thing to happen in my remote life. I posted jokes, memes, and quick answers to the occasional questions from colleagues. I was hilarious, and I was sure every one of my coworkers appreciated my energy and enthusiasm. It took about a week for the fun to fade. Soon, other, less humorous people started adding jokes that were not very funny (mostly annoying, really). The occasional questions from colleagues turned into unending interruptions to my normally productive work time. What was worse was that my answers or quick discussions often contained important information. When my team had to go back and try to find the information, we found ourselves scrolling through irrelevant memes, lame attempts at humor, and random conversations. Our intra-office chat turned from a unifying channel of connection into a series of hard-to-follow interruptions.

Informal communication channels can be important tools to build team cohesiveness and help solve the problem of having to wait days for a response to a quick, easy question. But when they aren't organized, they can make everyone's lives way more complicated.

Here are a few ideas to help declutter your communication channels:

- **Assess.** As each new tool is introduced and adopted by your team, take the time to consider not only what it adds, but also what it takes away. With that framework, you can best decide how to use the tool. Regularly evaluate adopted tools to determine whether the benefits they provide outweigh the costs.

- **Create clear labels and purposes for the channels.** For each channel, clearly define what type of information will be discussed. For instance, a channel may be project-specific or "general announcements" or "social chat." Try to make sure there aren't overlapping channels that make it unclear which channel to choose.

- **Establish norms.** By explicitly agreeing how the tools should be used, managers can make sure there is a balance between the benefits of using technology and the drawbacks of relying on it too heavily. For instance, teams may decide that for non-vital issues, asynchronous communication is preferable to synchronous meetings, or maybe that certain channels should require certain response times.

- **Set quiet hours.** Encourage employees to **turn off notifications** outside working hours. You may also want to designate specific times during the week for uninterrupted work.

✔ Virtual Tip

Archive old threads: Whether it's email or a messaging platform, clearing out rarely used threads boosts efficiency. It reduces clutter, helps employees find the right place to post, and ensures key information doesn't get buried. Archiving keeps the focus on what matters most.

Hardware Matters: Don't Let Bad Equipment Erode Trust

Remote employees can't do great work with subpar equipment. Yet, according to a 2021 CraftJack study, **38 percent of remote employees** work from their **bed**.[5] Settling for makeshift tools and equipment will certainly have a negative impact on productivity and the physical well-being of remote employees.

And don't underestimate how poor hardware impacts trust. When we work with old equipment, have inadequate support for the equipment we do have, or find ourselves required to use our own money to make the remote option workable, there is a clear message being received from the organization: *You are not important enough for us to support you.*

Equipping our remote workforce is yet one more way we can communicate value and trust. If you wouldn't ask an in-office employee to buy their own desk, don't expect a remote employee to fund their own office setup.

Tech should support, not distract. The best remote teams aren't the ones with the most tools—they're the ones who use their tools well. If you want your team to thrive:

- Choose tools that create clarity, not confusion.

- Encourage boundaries to prevent burnout.

- Equip employees with everything they need to succeed.

AMPLIFY COMMUNICATION

CLARIFY DIRECTION

BUILD PREDICTABILITY

REDEFINE ACCOUNTABILITY

CREATE CONNECTIONS

EQUIP YOUR PEOPLE

Equipping Benchmark Survey

Where does your team need the most support? Take a moment to evaluate where you excel and where additional training might be needed. The best training programs are not just one-time workshops—they are ongoing strategies that provide continuous support.

Use Table 3 to assess key skills and prioritize areas for development. Involve employees in the process to ensure training aligns with real needs rather than assumptions. Once you've completed this survey, identify the **top three** most critical areas and **get started**.

Table 3. Remote Management Skill Survey

WE'RE GOOD HERE	WE COULD USE SOME HELP	THIS IS A TOTAL TRAIN WRECK	REMOTE MANAGEMENT SKILL
			Creating buy-in with other managers and senior leaders regarding the value of remote work
			Reading nonverbal cues (understanding what lies between the lines)
			Facilitating collaborative remote meetings
			Emotional intelligence and remote emotional intelligence
			Dealing with remote assumptions and biases
			Clearly communicating information
			Team building

WE'RE GOOD HERE	WE COULD USE SOME HELP	THIS IS A TOTAL TRAIN WRECK	REMOTE MANAGEMENT SKILL
			Providing employee support in a remote environment
			Active listening skills
			The new digital language (emojis, punctuation, timing, dedicated channels)
			Communicating and reinforcing Mission, Values, and Priorities
			Managing employee check-ins and giving regular feedback
			Providing negative feedback and holding employees accountable
			Empowering and motivating remote employees
			Establishing clear expectations
			Supporting remote employees' career growth
			Making wise choices in adopting new technologies

AMPLIFY COMMUNICATION

CLARIFY DIRECTION

BUILD PREDICTABILITY

REDEFINE ACCOUNTABILITY

CREATE CONNECTIONS

EQUIP YOUR PEOPLE

 **Virtual Tip**

Create a core remote office setup: Standardize the equipment list for every remote employee. This may include a laptop, monitor, headset, microphone, and webcam. Additional equipment like lighting, a standing desk, or an ergonomic chair may also be part of your remote work offerings.

Final Thought:
The Right Tools Build Trust

Equipping remote employees isn't just about technology—it's about empowering them to succeed. When organizations thoughtfully invest in their remote workforce through training programs, career development opportunities, and cutting-edge tools, they're not merely providing resources—they're demonstrating commitment to their employees' professional fulfillment and overall job satisfaction.

Don't overlook the key takeaways:

- **Training creates confidence.** Employees who receive ongoing skill development are more engaged, productive, and innovative.

- **Career growth aids retention.** Employees who feel supported in their professional development are more likely to stay.

- **The right tools eliminate barriers.** Technology should enhance efficiency, not create frustration.

By investing in training, career growth, and proper tools, you build a workforce that is competent, motivated, and committed—the foundation of trust at a distance.

Trust doesn't happen by accident—especially at a distance. It takes intention, clarity, and a leader committed to showing up, even when the office disappears

---

Presence isn't
proximity, it
is intentional
connection. Make
the commute
worth it.

NEGOTIATING THE
IN-PERSON DILEMMA
Leverage the face-to-face office with in-person opportunities.

It seems like every company is trying to figure out *how*, *when*, and *if* employees should return to the office. Even as we put the finishing touches on this book, there are daily headlines about companies implementing various degrees of RTO policies and experimenting with creative hybrid approaches.

A recent Gallup poll suggests hybrid approaches have become an increasingly preferred option:

- Six in ten employees with remote-capable jobs want a hybrid work arrangement.

- About a third prefer fully remote work.

- Less than 10 percent prefer to work on-site full time.[1]

It makes sense. A hybrid approach can help employees manage those deficits in *information* and *relationships* that a fully remote environment may create while still allowing for autonomy and flexibility.

But here is the key to creating *successful* hybrid solutions: **Trust doesn't magically develop just because people come into the office.** Whether remote or face-to-face, trust still requires amplified communication, clear direction, predictability, accountable autonomy, connection, and support. It may look different in remote settings, but it still takes intentional management.

If you are going to the trouble of requiring reluctant workers to come back to the office, you **have** to make it worthwhile for them and for you. Be intentional about using those in-office days to connect, support, and innovate—together.

Finding the Right Hybrid Solution

If your company is still refining its remote/in-person balance, it's helpful to analyze the strengths and weaknesses of common hybrid models.

Ways to Organize Hybrid Work

There are five main models for organizing hybrid work,[2] each with distinct pros and cons:

1. **Office-first.** Most of the work is done in the in-person office. Only rare exceptions are made for those who need to work from home on an ad hoc basis.

   + Communication is more natural and spontaneous.

   + It is easier to directly supervise employees.

   − Employees will most likely desire increased flexibility and autonomy, and the organization is limited to hiring employees who live nearby.

   − A recent Gallup poll suggests that this option produces the **least** amount of employee engagement.[3]

2. **Flexible hybrid.** Employees have great discretion in deciding when to work off-site and when to come into the office.

   + Employees have flexibility and autonomy; they can choose which projects are best worked on in which environment.

   + Employees feel that they are trusted and their expertise is valued.

+ The environment is aligned with the person and the task.

− It becomes difficult to plan when and where people will be available.

− Utilization of space becomes complicated, especially if office space has been minimized to leverage the savings that can result from the decreasing in-office workforce.

− Very clear policies are required to make sure there is fairness across teams.

3. **Team-designated hybrid.** Each team has the ability to decide when, how, and where they work together.

+ The location will be dependent on the project, making best use of in-person and remote environments.

+ Autonomy is underscored, as teams are trusted to make good decisions.

− While promoting team cohesiveness, this approach also reinforces silos and an us/them mentality.

− Teams don't always agree, and team members may have different needs.

− This approach makes management extremely complex, with different kinds of approaches for each team.

4. **Remote-first.** Most, if not all, employees work remotely. There may be some office space available for occasional team meetings and conferences.

+ Organizations have the ability to hire talent from around the world.

+ Employee flexibility and autonomy are highlighted.

+ When strategies to build trust at a distance are implemented, productivity and satisfaction will remain high.

− Communication and culture building require commitment and intentionality.

- A new management mindset is needed, focusing on results, not hours worked.
- There still exists a need to rent or own some sort of in-person office space for special projects or events.

5. **Set schedule.** With employee collaboration, a schedule is created where some or all of the employees come into the office on certain days of the week.

   + This approach provides structure and predictability.
   + Having a set schedule helps teams establish a rhythm that balances in-person and remote work.
   + Office space usage can be optimized to save costs.
   - Certain teams may never be in the office at the same time, limiting collaboration.
   - Rigid schedules may not accommodate evolving project needs.

Who Should Decide on the Right Hybrid Model?

Making the decision about which hybrid model to implement collectively can actually help build trust. A 2024 Gallup poll suggests that allowing a team to decide on which policy will work best for them has the biggest positive impact on collaboration and feelings of fairness, with top-down decisions perceived as least fair.[4] That being said, when the executive leadership team creates work policies, it can ensure there is conformity and fairness across the organization and address emerging pain points by regularly assessing those policies, taking into account changing employee needs and evolving industry best practices.[5]

There's no perfect hybrid model, but the most successful organizations **listen to their people** and **stay flexible** as they refine their work-from-home strategies.

Make the Office Count

There is little doubt that technology helps us do some things extremely well—often better than if we were all sitting next to each other in a traditional office. But other tasks simply benefit from being done together.

Unfortunately, we have seen too many hybrid offices where workers make the frustrating commute into the office only to sit in an isolated cubicle that doesn't even belong to them, doing the same tasks they could be doing from home.

We can do better. The real power of hybrid work comes from thoughtful planning—choosing the right tasks for the right space. Here are some things to consider:

REMOTE WORK IS BEST FOR

- **One-way information sharing.** Use email, video calls, or prerecorded messages.

- **Solo work that requires deep focus.** Allow employees to concentrate at home.

- **Quick check-ins.** Keep them short and consistent over video.

IN-PERSON WORK IS BEST FOR

- **Brainstorming, problem solving, and innovation.** Collaboration is easier face to face.

- **Building relationships and strengthening teams.** Leverage social events and casual interactions to build important connections.

- **Providing hands-on training.** Just-in-time learning and immediate feedback are more effective in person.

- **Difficult or sensitive conversations.** When emotions run high, in-person meetings foster understanding, taking into account all of the social and emotional information that gets lost with reduced nonverbal communication.

If you're bringing people into the office, make sure it's for work that actually benefits from being done in person.

The Hidden Challenge: Proximity Bias

Hybrid workplaces offer flexibility and opportunity, but they also come with a hidden risk: in-person employees get more attention. We naturally gravitate toward those who are physically present. It's easier to chat casually, collaborate spontaneously, and build trust with colleagues who are sitting next to us. But this can create an uneven playing field.

According to a recent Slack study:

- Black, Hispanic, and Asian American workers are more likely to work remotely than their white colleagues.

- Women are more likely to choose remote work than men.[7]

A study by researchers at Stanford University showed that remote workers were 13 percent more productive than in-person employees, but only half as likely to be promoted.[8] If managers unknowingly favor in-person employees for promotions, assignments, or mentorship, they may inadvertently sideline underrepresented groups. It's human nature that managers will promote the people they know best—but it is also a problem, especially in blended workplaces.

A trusted leader needs to take steps to ensure promotions and raises are decided equitably:

- Use clear, measurable performance standards rather than subjective "visibility."
- Make sure remote employees have mentorship opportunities.
- Recognize and reward contributions equally, whether made in-person or online.

Proximity bias is one of the greatest challenges of the hybrid workplace. Maintaining the equity promised by the remote or hybrid work environment requires a conscious choice to reach out to our remote workers. Here are a few final practices to consider:

- Schedule **more** one-on-one time with remote employees.
- Be intentional about including remote workers in discussions. Call on them during hybrid meetings.
- Assign structured roles to remote team members so they stay engaged, particularly in video meetings.
- Track promotion and development opportunities to ensure remote employees aren't overlooked.

✔ Virtual Tip

Confront proximity bias: Don't assume in-person employees are more committed.

Hybrid options can solve many of the challenges of remote work, but if not adequately managed, they will create a two-tiered system where remote workers suffer. Bottom line: If you have both remote and in-person employees, you need to **spend more time supporting your remote workers** to level the playing field.

The Changing Relevance of Trust

Trust is undergoing significant change. Long ago, people distrusted others for one of two reasons: unfamiliarity ("I don't know you," "You look and sound different from me," or "You live on the other side of the mountain") or familiarity ("I know how you act; therefore, I don't trust you").

Eventually, trust became *institutional.* We could distrust a single senator yet still believe in the government, or question one teacher while maintaining faith in the education system. But a few decades ago, institutional trust in the U.S. began to erode. In 1958, around 73 percent of Americans trusted the government to do what was right "just about always" or "most of the time." By 2024, that number had dropped to just **22 percent,** with only 2 percent saying "just about always."[9]

Media fragmentation and increasing reliance on technology have played a major role in the ongoing decrease in *societal* trust— *the* news became *my* news and *your* news, with deepfakes, fake reviews, and digital manipulation further complicating matters.

As trust declines across all levels of society, human presence becomes not only more powerful, but more essential than ever before.

Humans Need Humans

As powerful as remote work can be, at the end of the day, we're more than digital images on a screen. **We're people.** No matter how advanced our virtual tools become, we still need **real-life** human connection. Sometimes we simply need to breathe the same air, see the same reality, and exist in the same space. Human presence is powerful.

As we work to develop remote strategies that recreate social presence within a virtual space, we have to agree that communication mediated by technology is simply not the same. We still need to find time to **be** together. People just work better that way.

In-person experiences—whether they're regular workshops, quarterly training days, or biannual retreats—energize remote work. These physical meetups serve to jump-start relationships, strengthen organizational culture, and build trust in ways that have a direct and long-lasting impact on the remote workplace. Trust at a distance is fueled by real-life communication. Whatever tomorrow's workplace looks like, we can't underestimate our need for real-life, person-to-person interaction.

 **Virtual Tip**

Count the cost: As you calculate the *cost savings* of remote work, it's vital to factor in the *added costs* of in-person events.

Next Steps to Building Trust at a Distance

1. Assess your trust gaps:

- ❑ What's your biggest challenge in building trust remotely?
- ❑ Which area needs the most focus—communication, direction, predictability, accountability, connection, or equipping your team?
- ❑ How well are you addressing the unique challenges of remote and hybrid work?

Trust starts with awareness.

2. Choose one key action to implement this week:

Amplify Communication:

- ❑ Ask clarifying questions at the end of your next meeting to make sure everyone is on the same page.
- ❑ The next time you feel frustrated, engage curiosity instead of certainty.

Clarify Direction:

- ❑ Reinforce your organization's Mission, Values, and Priorities in everyday conversation.
- ❑ Tell a mission story at the beginning of your next meeting.

Increase Predictability:

- ❑ Set up a one-on-one check-in schedule.
- ❑ Schedule one office hour every week.

Redefine Accountability:

- ❑ Shift from tracking hours to measuring outcomes.
- ❑ Follow up the next project with a team feedback session.
- ❑ Ask for feedback on *your* performance.

Strengthen Connection:

- ❑ Plan a team-building activity (virtual or in-person).
- ❑ The next time someone asks you how you are doing, *tell them*.

Equip Your People:

- ❑ Identify one training gap and address it.
- ❑ Find someone to mentor.

Big changes start with small, consistent actions.

3. Commit to trust-based leadership:

The best leaders don't demand trust—they earn it. That means:

- ❑ Showing up consistently
- ❑ Leading with clarity
- ❑ Listening actively
- ❑ Empowering autonomy
- ❑ Prioritizing relationships

Trust is the *ultimate* competitive advantage!

Final Thought: The Workplace Has Changed— Trust Must Change with It

The future of work isn't fully remote. It isn't fully in-person. *It's adaptive.* Some companies will thrive in a remote-first model. Others will leverage hybrid structures. Some will bring all employees back to the office full time. Thanks to emerging technologies and artificial intelligence, what tomorrow's workplace looks like is a little hard to imagine. Yet, one thing is clear: The organizations that succeed will be the ones that build trust—at a distance, in person, and everywhere in between.

The world is watching. Now is your time to lead.

TRUST AT A DISTANCE

DISCUSSION GUIDE

Use this discussion guide with your team to prompt thoughtful conversations about building trust at a distance.

It's a Whole New Day

1. Begin the conversation by talking about your current attitudes related to remote work:

    - What do you enjoy about remote work?

    - What are the problems you have found?

    Have everyone share an example of each.

2. What are the biggest challenges your organization currently faces related to remote work?

3. Dream big. As a group, create a vision for what a great remote workplace would look like for your organization.

Strategy 1: Amplify Communication

1. Go around the group and identify which of the following communication practices you do well and which need the most work:

    Clarity:

    - I am careful to provide enough information to communicate my intended message.

    - I am attuned to what information gets lost without nonverbal cues.

Respect:

- I try to reply to messages in a timely manner (even messages from junior reports).

- I respond to intra-office chats with enough length to get my message across.

Silos:

- I actively create ways for teams to communicate with one another.

Norms:

- Our team has clearly defined what communication channels should be used for what tasks. We also have clarified expectations for each channel (email, video, intra-office text).

Assumptions:

- I intentionally pay attention to the assumptions I make.

- I actively ask questions when I am upset or frustrated.

2. Discuss why each of these points is both important *and* challenging for your team.

Strategy 2: Clarify Direction

1. As a group, discuss the clarity and appropriateness of your organizational Mission, Values, and Priorities. If you aren't sure what they are, where to find them, or what they mean, the first step is to take some time to make sure these elements are clear.

2. Spend a few minutes telling each other something you appreciate about each member, and then connect that attribute to a value. Use this exercise as a reminder of how to work MVPs into normal conversation.

3. How well does your team understand how their work fits in with the organizational MVPs? Brainstorm ways you can help employees establish priorities and explicitly align them with the MVPs. Give examples of past successes and failures.

Strategy 3: Build Predictability

1. Give an example of a successful check-in you have recently had with an employee.

   How often do these kinds of check-ins happen?

   What made it "successful"?

   Is there a structure you can use for *every* check-in, to ensure that you

   - Listen to employees' challenges?

   - Help employees solve problems?

   - Work with employees to set priorities?

   - Support and acknowledge good work?

2. What is your biggest challenge with regard to establishing routine check-ins with your team?

Strategy 4: Redefine Accountability

1. List what you see as some of the benefits of employee autonomy and discuss them as a group.

2. Identify ways you can further empower your employees to make their own choices in a way that supports the work of the team.

3. Share strategies you have used to move from measuring time worked to results produced. Make sure to provide examples. Also talk about what worked with each strategy and what needs to be improved.

4. Talk about the last time you gave someone feedback (whether positive or negative) on their performance. How did it go? How could you improve your feedback practice for next time?

Strategy 5: Create Connections

1. Reflect on which of these video practices you do well and which ones you need to pay more attention to:

   - Commit to really paying attention to your employees and team members.

   - Look at the person you are talking to on video.

   - Notice what is not being said, monitoring nonverbal cues.

   - Practice active listening—for example, use nonverbal cues such as smiles and nods, and ask clarifying and summarizing questions.

   Share your thoughts with the group.

2. In your group, discuss the benefits and drawbacks of sharing information with your team that is a little more personal in nature. What are some lessons you have learned in your career related to sharing personal information?

3. Discuss ideas you have, or programs you have heard about, related to community building at a distance. Establish at least one or two plans for how you can enhance the social connections within your team.

4. Share a time (either in a remote or an in-person setting) where you have seen bad social behavior. Consider:

   - What do you think caused the drama?

   - How did you (or could you) deal with the issue?

   - How might these behaviors be more difficult to manage in a remote workplace?

Strategy 6: Equip Your People

1. Share both positive and negative experiences you have had with online training. Consider:

    - What worked?

    - What definitely did *not* work?

    - What types of training work best online, and what works best face to face?

2. Share examples of how you built your career. As a group:

    - Identify which career development steps seem to be most impactful.

    - Discuss how these steps might be adapted to the remote workplace.

3. Share insights you have, or lessons learned, related to each of these commonly used tools:

    - Videoconferencing platforms

    - Project management software

    - Intra-office communication channels

    - Any other helpful (or not helpful) remote workplace tools

Negotiating the In-Person Dilemma

1. If you work in a hybrid setting, share examples of times when you have noticed a proximity bias. How have you compensated for the disadvantage of working remotely?

2. Discuss the benefits of gathering all your remote workers together for a face-to-face event:

    - What specific goals might you have for the in-person time?

    - What strategies can you use to leverage tasks that are best done in person?

Notes

It's a Whole New Day

1 NJIT, "Benefits of Remote Work," accessed May 5, 2025, https://hr.njit.edu/benefits-remote-work.

2 Danielle Kost, "You're Right! You Are Working Longer and Attending More Meetings," Harvard Business School Working Knowledge, September 14, 2020, https://www.library.hbs.edu/working-knowledge/you-re-right-you-are-working-longer-and-attending-more-meetings.

3 GitLab, "The Annual Remote Work Report by GitLab: There's a New Status Quo," press release, April 27, 2021, https://about.gitlab.com/press/releases/2021-04-27-annual-gitlab-remote-work-report/.

4 Cevat Giray Aksoy et al., "Time Savings When Working from Home," National Bureau of Economic Research working paper 30866, January 2023, https://www.nber.org/system/files/working_papers/w30866/w30866.pdf.

5 Yanqiu Tao et al., "Climate Mitigation Potentials of Teleworking Are Sensitive to Changes in Lifestyle and Workplace Rather Than ICT Usage," *Proceedings of the National Academy of Sciences* 120, no. 39 (2023): e2304099120, https://doi.org/10.1073/pnas.2304099120.

6 Aleksandr Volodarsky, "Research: Startups Save up to $10,601,000 Yearly on Remote Workers," *Lemon.io*, October 10, 2024, https://lemon.io/blog/research-startups-save-up-to-10601000-yearly-on-remote-workers/.

7 Chris Salviati, "Remote Worker Migration Expected to Persist in 2023," Apartment List, February 6, 2023, https://www.apartmentlist.com/research/remote-worker-migration-expected-to-persist-in-2023.

8 ReacHIRE, "The Impact of Remote Work on Inclusion, Diversity, and Retention," *ReacHIRE Blog*, August 30, 2023, https://www.reachire.com/blog/the-impact-of-remote-work-on-inclusion-diversity-and-retention/.

9 Jeffrey Howard, "The Benefits of Remote Work for People with Disabilities," InclusionHub, March 22, 2022, https://www.inclusionhub.com/articles/benefits-of-remote-work.

10 Patrick Riley, interview by David Horsager, video call, November 11, 2024.

11 Patrick Riley interview.

12 Ashley Reichheld and Amelia Dunlop, "How to Build a High-Trust Workplace," *MIT Sloan Management Review*, January 24, 2023, https://sloanreview.mit.edu/article/how-to-build-a-high-trust-workplace/.

13 Trust Edge Leadership Institute, *2022 Trust Outlook: Global Research Study*, April 2022, https://trustedge.com/the-research/, 18.

14 Paul J. Zak, "The Neuroscience of Trust," American Association for Physician Leadership, November 8, 2023, https://www.physicianleaders.org/articles/the-neuroscience-of-trust.

15 GLINT and HR.com, *The State of Employee Engagement in 2018*, March 2018, https://info.glintinc.com/rs/586-OTD-288/images/The_State_of_Employee_Engagement_in_2018_Whitepaper_HRdotcom_Glint.pdf, 14.

16 C. Shawn Burke et al., "Trust in Leadership: A Multi-Level Review and Integration," *The Leadership Quarterly* 18, no. 6 (2007): 606–632, https://doi.org/10.1016/j.leaqua.2007.09.006.

17 Albert Mehrabian, *Silent Messages: Implicit Communication of Emotions and Attitudes* (Wadsworth, 1971), 43.

18 Judith A. Hall and Mark L. Knapp, eds. *Nonverbal Communication* (De Gruyter Mouton, 2013).

19 Bobby Herrera, interview by David Horsager, video call, December 4, 2024.

Strategy 1: Amplify Communication

1 Karen Mangia, interview by David Horsager, St. Paul, MN, April 14, 2025.

2 Brian Parkinson, "Emotions in Direct and Remote Social Interaction: Getting through the Spaces between Us," *Computers in Human Behavior* 24, no. 4 (2008): 1510–1529, https://doi.org/10.1016/j.chb.2007.05.006.

3 Erica Dhawan, *Digital Body Language: How to Build Trust and Connection, No Matter the Distance* (St. Martin's Press, 2021).

4 Dhawan, *Digital Body Language*, 24.

5 Douglas Stone et al., *Difficult Conversations: How to Discuss What Matters Most* (Penguin Books, 2010), 37.

6 Paige Hendrix Buckner, personal communication with Peggy Kendall, March 4, 2025.

Strategy 2: Clarify Direction

1 The "Rule of Seven" is a common marketing strategy originally developed in the 1930s, when advertisers found moviegoers needed to see a movie poster at least seven times before taking action. See Nicole Steffen, "The Timeless Power of the Marketing Rule of 7," *Insights Blog*, August 14, 2023, https://nicolesteffen.com/2023/09/12/the-timeless-power-of-the-marketing-rule-of-7/.

2 Starbucks, "Our Starbucks Mission," *Starbucks Stories & News*, January 9, 2025, accessed May 27, 2025, https://about.starbucks.com/stories/2025/our-starbucks-mission/.

3   Nathaniel Meyersohn, "Walmart Made Changes to Greeter Jobs at Stores. Workers with Disabilities Got Squeezed," *CNN Business*, March 1, 2019, https://www.cnn.com/2019/02/26/business/walmart-greeters.

4   David Horsager, *Trust Matters More Than Ever: 40 Tools to Lead Better, Grow Faster & Build Trust Now* (BroadStreet Publishing Group, 2024), 59.

5   Nathan Regier, interview by David Horsager, St. Paul, MN, December 10, 2024.

Strategy 3: Build Predictability

1   Jim Harter, "A Great Manager's Most Important Habit," Gallup, May 30, 2023, https://www.gallup.com/workplace/505370/great-manager-important-habit.aspx.

2   This is referring to the Scrum framework, which is a part of Agile project management. For more information, visit scrum.org.

3   Eric Mahler, interview by David Horsager, St. Paul, MN, December 12, 2024.

Strategy 4: Redefine Accountability

1   Jessica Mathews, "Better.com CEO Blasts Laid-Off Employees, Accusing Them of 'Stealing' by Working Only Two Hours Daily," *Fortune*, December 3, 2021, https://fortune.com/2021/12/03/better-com-ceo-attacks-laid-off-employees-blind-message-board/.

2   Kristin Schwab, "'Overemployed' People Secretly Work Overlapping Remote Jobs," *Marketplace*, October 23, 2023, https://www.marketplace.org/2023/10/23/overemployed-people-work-overlapping-remote-jobs/.

3   Dawn Allcot, "Americans Are Choosing to Be 'Over-Employed' Instead of Working Back-to-Back Jobs," *Yahoo! Finance*, October 30, 2022, https://finance.yahoo.com/news/americans-choosing-over-employed-instead-130836718.html.

4   Allcot, "Americans Are Choosing to Be 'Over-Employed'"

5   Chase E. Thiel et al., "Stripped of Agency: The Paradoxical Effect of Employee Monitoring on Deviance," *Journal of Management* 49, no. 2 (2021): 709–740, https://doi.org/10.1177/01492063211053224.

6   Chen-Bo Zhong, Vanessa K. Bohns, and Francesca Gino, "Good Lamps Are the Best Police: Darkness Increases Dishonesty and Self-Interested Behavior," *Psychological Science* 21, no. 3 (2010): 311–314, https://doi.org/10.1177/0956797609360754.

7   Check out Kudoboard (kudoboard.com), or create something similar yourself.

8   Daniel H. Pink, *Drive: The Surprising Truth about What Motivates Us* (Riverhead Books, 2009).

9   Allan Lee, Sara Willis, and Amy Wei Tian, "When Empowering Employ-
    ees Works, and When It Doesn't," *Harvard Business Review*, March 2,
    2018, https://hbr.org/2018/03/when-empowering-employees-works
    -and-when-it-doesnt.

10 Anthony Diekemper, interview by David Horsager, video call, Janu-
    ary 21, 2025.

11 David Streitfeld, "The Long, Unhappy History of Working from
    Home," *The New York Times*, June 29, 2020, https://www.nytimes.com
    /2020/06/29/technology/working-from-home-failure.html.

12 Joe Kimbell, interview by David Horsager, St. Paul, MN, February 15,
    2025.

Strategy 5: Create Connections

1   U.S. Department of Health and Human Services, *Our Epidemic of Loneli-
    ness and Isolation: The U.S. Surgeon General's Advisory on the Healing Effects
    of Social Connection and Community* (HHS, 2023), https://www.hhs.gov
    /sites/default/files/surgeon-general-social-connection-advisory.pdf, 13.

2   U.S. Department of Health and Human Services, *Our Epidemic of
    Loneliness*.

3   Einar H. Dyvik, "Loneliness among Employees Working from Home
    Worldwide 2023," Statista, December 10, 2024, https://www.statista
    .com/statistics/1476817/global-employee-lineliness-wfh/#statistic
    Container.

4   Debbie Gray, interview by Peggy Kendall, St. Paul, MN, December 15,
    2024.

5   Rachel Montañez, "Fighting Loneliness on Remote Teams," *Harvard
    Business Review*, March 22, 2024, https://hbr.org/2024/03/fighting
    -loneliness-on-remote-teams.

6   Paul E. Funk III, interview by David Horsager, video call, Decem-
    ber 5, 2024.

7   Adriana Cacoveanu, "How to Build a Strong Workplace Community,"
    YAROOMS Blog, October 25, 2022, https://www.yarooms.com/blog
    /how-to-build-a-strong-workplace-community.

8   Christine Porath and Carla Piñeyro Sublett, "Rekindling a Sense
    of Community at Work," *Harvard Business Review*, August 26, 2022,
    https://hbr.org/2022/08/rekindling-a-sense-of-community-at-work.

9   Montañez, "Fighting Loneliness."

10 Ernest G. Bormann, *Effective Small Group Communication* (Burgess
    International Group, 1996).

11 DiSC is a registered trademark of John Wiley & Sons, Inc.

12 CliftonStrengths and StrengthsFinder are registered trademarks of
    Gallup, Inc.

13 Martin Lea and Russell Spears, "Computer-Mediated Communication, De-Individuation and Group Decision-Making," *International Journal of Man-Machine Studies* 34, no. 2 (1991): 283–301, https://doi.org/10.1016 /0020-7373(91)90045-9.

14 Anthony Diekemper, interview by David Horsager, video call, January 21, 2025.

15 Lucy Meakin, "Remote Working's Longer Hours Are New Normal for Many," *Bloomberg*, February 2, 2021, https://www.bloomberg.com /news/articles/2021-02-02/remote-working-s-longer-hours-are-new -normal-for-many-chart.

16 Nicholas A. Bloom et al., "Does Working from Home Work? Evidence from a Chinese Experiment," National Bureau of Economic Research working paper 18871, March 2013, https://www.nber.org /system/files/working_papers/w18871/w18871.pdf.

17 Mitja Puppis, "The Impact of Remote Work Burnout: Statistics, Causes, and Effective Solutions," My Hours, August 10, 2024, https:// myhours.com/articles/the-impact-of-remote-work-burnout-statistics -causes-and-effective-solutions-2; Kapo Wong, Alan H. S. Chan, and S. C. Ngan, "The Effect of Long Working Hours and Overtime on Occupational Health: A Meta-Analysis of Evidence from 1998 to 2018," *International Journal of Environmental Research and Public Health* 16, no. 12 (2019): 2102, https://doi.org/10.3390/ijerph16122102.

Strategy 6: Equip Your People

1 Robin, *Productivity and Proximity in the Hybrid Workplace* (Robin, 2023), https://robinpowered.com/reports/productivity-and-proximity, 2.

2 Adobe Communications Team, "Adobe Future Workforce Study: What U.S. Employers Need to Know about Gen Z in the Workplace," *Adobe Blog*, September 27, 2023, https://blog.adobe.com/en/publish /2023/09/27/adobe-future-workforce-study-what-us-employers -need-know-about-gen-z-workplace.

3 Neil Postman, "Five Things We Need to Know about Technological Change" (speech, Denver, CO, March 28, 1998), https://www.cs .ucdavis.edu/~rogaway/classes/188/materials/postman.pdf.

4 Vignesh Ramachandran, "Stanford Researchers Identify Four Causes for 'Zoom Fatigue' and Their Simple Fixes," *Stanford Report*, February 23, 2021, https://news.stanford.edu/stories/2021/02/four -causes-zoom-fatigue-solutions.

5 Erica Pandey, "Stat of the Day: 38% of Remote Workers Work from Bed," *Axios*, July 29, 2021, https://www.axios.com/2021/07/29/38 -percent-remote-workers-work-bed.

Negotiating the In-Person Dilemma

1 Gallup, "Hybrid Work," accessed April 5, 2025, https://www.gallup.com/401384/indicator-hybrid-work.aspx.

2 Energage, "Types of Hybrid Work Models," Top Workplaces, June 29, 2023, https://topworkplaces.com/types-of-hybrid-work-models.

3 Gallup, "Hybrid Work"

4 Gallup, "Hybrid Work"

5 Kaya Ismail, "Does Your Hybrid Work Policy Need a Revision?" *Reworked*, January 31, 2023, https://www.reworked.co/digital-workplace/does-your-hybrid-work-policy-need-a-revision/.

6 Mike Waddick, interview by David Horsager, video call, December 12, 2024.

7 HRD Connect, "Making Hybrid Work for Everyone: How Slack Is Fighting Proximity Bias," April 19, 2022, https://www.hrdconnect.com/casestudy/making-hybrid-work-for-everyone-how-slack-is-fighting-proximity-bias/.

8 Nicholas A. Bloom et al., "Does Working from Home Work? Evidence from a Chinese Experiment," National Bureau of Economic Research working paper 18871, March 2013, https://www.nber.org/system/files/working_papers/w18871/w18871.pdf, 3.

9 Pew Research Center, "Public Trust in Government: 1958–2024," June 24, 2024, https://www.pewresearch.org/politics/2024/06/24/public-trust-in-government-1958-2024/.

Acknowledgments

A huge thank you to the countless **leaders, teams, and organizations** who have shared their insights, challenges, and successes with us. Your stories and experiences have shaped the ideas in this book.

To the **executives, managers, and employees** navigating the new workplace landscape—you are pioneers. Thank you for your commitment to building workplaces where trust, performance, and people thrive.

To our **families and teams**—thank you for your unwavering support as we wrote this book. We couldn't have done this work if it wasn't for our team at Berrett-Koehler and our grace-filled, patient, and supportive production manager, Heidi Sheard. Our reviewers, including Scott Allison and Joel Rude, were kind and invaluable in helping us focus our message.

And finally, to **you, the reader**: By investing in trust, you are investing in the future of leadership. Thank you for joining us on this journey. Together, we will build workplaces that work—for everyone.

Index

mindset
    for accountable autonomy, 78
    changing your, 12, 15
    problem-solving, 74
misalignment, 35, 58
mission
    alignment, 33, 35
    mission moments, 46
    in MVP framework, 37–41
    reminders about, 45
    as the "why," 37–38
Mission, Values, and Priorities
    (MVP)
    assessing your, 42
    clarity via, 49
    framework overview, 37–41
    in-person meetings about, 48
    reminders about, 44, 45
    stories to reinforce, 46
mistakes, admitting, 92–93
misunderstanding, reducing, 27
Monday kickoff meetings, 62
motivation, 34, 69, 93

N

narratives, self-told, 28, 30
neutrality, 16
Next Element Consulting, 49
nonverbal cues, 1, 2, 11, 23, 88, 91
notification fatigue, 116, 120

O

office-first hybrids, 128
office hours, 57
on-the-fly learning, 110–111
"open door" myth, 18, 30, 56
Oxford University, 23

P

partners, work, 62
passivity vs. intentionality, 30
Patton, Bruce, 28
performance
    addressing poor, 81–82
    and availability, 31

and clear priorities, 40
    feedback on, 80–81
    training to support, 106–107
    trust as key to, 1, 10
    values-based, 39
personality types, 9, 73
poor performance, 81–82
Populus Group, 13
positive tone, 25
Postman, Neil, 115
praise, 69, 80, 97
predictability, building
    assessing your, 54–55, 141
    assurance via, 52
    via consistent check-ins, 53,
        57–62
    and inevitable change, 51
    as key to remote trust, 5
priorities
    competing, 34, 35, 40
    in MVP framework, 40, 41
    Priority Alignment tool, 47–48
    top-three daily, 102
problem-solving mindset, 74
productivity
    autonomy and, 71
    via clear priorities, 40
    connection/productivity
        balance, 97
    equipment and, 105
    leader concerns about, 65–67
    remote work and increased, 7,
        101–102, 132
    via trust, 1
project management software,
    115–116
promotions for in-office work, 111,
    112, 133
proximity bias, 132–133
Punch Through, 132
punctuation, 24–25

Q

questions
    clarification via, 20, 92

clear channels for, 55
structured check-ins for, 61

R

Regier, Nate, 49
relationship-building
    challenges of remote, 11
    creating connections, 5
    importance of, 94
    via paying attention, 90–92
    via sharing, 92–93
    See also connections, creating
reliability, flexibility and, 74
remote-first hybrids, 129
Remote Rising Leaders initiative, 112
remote workplaces
    choice in, 72, 73
    clarity in, 36
    community at, 95
    hidden landmines in, 52–53
    invisibility in, 111–112, 113
    lack of information in, 11, 63
    lack of on-the-fly learning,
        110–111
    lack of trust in, 1
    learning opportunities in, 106
    loneliness of, 86, 87
    mindsets about, 12
    misalignment in, 33
    mission as key for, 38
    multiple remote jobs, 66
    open commitment to, 13
    opportunities of, 3–4, 7–9, 10,
        13, 131
    overcommunication in, 17,
        23–24
    proximity bias vs., 132–133
    remote/in-person balance, 128
    standard equipment for, 124
    support in, 56
    technological proficiency
        in, 108
    tensions unique to, 2
    training for, 107–108
    trust in, 4–5, 10

    unsupervised work in, 9
    and work-life boundaries,
        101–102
repetition, 37, 45
replies, speed of, 24–25, 27
response, length of, 24–25
responsibility, personal, 39
results-driven leadership, 78
retention, employee, 9, 94,
    111, 112
return-to-office (RTO) mandates,
    9, 127
rewards, team-based, 97
Roxie AI, 22

S

safety, psychological, 92
Scrum calls, 63
security, 109
self-assessments
    of accountability, 76–77, 141
    of clear directions, 42–43, 140
    of connections, 142
    of equipment needs, 122–123,
        143
    of in-person workplaces, 143
    about predictability, 54–55, 141
    about remote work, 14–15
    of trust gaps, 136–137
    of your communication, 20–21,
        139
self-discipline, 109
sharing, 92–93
silence, 16, 18–19, 50
siloed communication, 26,
    36, 140
sitting vs. standing, 119
skills-gap analyses, 108
social capital, 111, 113
social identity deindividuation
    effects (SIDE) model, 98–99
Soderquist, Don, 46
software, 115–116
sponsorship, 114
standing vs. sitting, 119

U

uncertainty, 52
University of Toronto, 69
University of Wyoming, 67

V

values, organizational, 38–39, 41, 44
videoconferencing, 20, 117–119
video recordings, asynchronous, 22
virtual workplaces. *See* remote
   workplaces
vulnerability, 31, 92–93

W

Waddick, Mike, 132
Walmart, 46

"why," mission as the, 37–38
word choice
   digital tone, 24–25
   language for mission, 38
work–life boundaries, 101–102
workplaces
   21st century changes to, 7, 12,
      13, 138
   employer doubts of remote, 9
   optimizing, 9
World of Travel, 79

Z

Zak, Paul, 10
Zoom fatigue, 117–119

About the Authors

David Horsager, DLitt, CSP, CPAE, is the world's leading authority on trust. Researcher, keynote speaker, and bestselling author of four books, including *Trust Matters More Than Ever: 40 Proven Trust Tools to Lead Better, Grow Faster & Build Trust Now*, he has spent decades studying how trust impacts individuals, teams, and organizations—transforming the way leaders operate in today's fast-changing world.

David is the CEO of Trust Edge Leadership Institute, the inventor of the Enterprise Trust Index™, and the director of the global study Trust Outlook®. His expertise has earned him accolades, including being named a Senior Fellow at Indiana Wesleyan University, a Certified Speaking Professional (CSP & CPAE), and an inductee into the National Speakers Hall of Fame—a designation held by an elite group of speakers worldwide.

David's insights on trust have been featured in *Forbes*, *The Wall Street Journal*, *Fast Company*, and *Harvard Business Review*. He has advised and trained leaders at some of the world's most respected organizations, including Delta Airlines, McDonald's, FedEx, Toyota, Walmart, Zoom, MIT, the New York Yankees, and even global governments. Learn more at DavidHorsager.com.

Peggy Kendall, PhD, has dedicated over thirty years to researching, teaching, and writing about technology, communication, and leadership. As a professor of communication studies at Bethel University in St. Paul, MN, she has helped thousands of undergraduate and graduate students, and business professionals, become better communicators and leaders.

A Fulbright scholar, ICF-certified coach, and organizational consultant, Peggy specializes in examining the impact of technology on how we think, communicate, and connect. Her extensive research has led to three books and multiple articles on digital communication, workplace culture, and the evolving nature of leadership in a tech-driven world.

Peggy has spoken at conferences across the country, delivering engaging and insightful keynotes to audiences ranging from middle schoolers to Fortune 500 executives. She works with organizations to improve workplace culture, strengthen team dynamics, and develop high-trust environments that foster collaboration and innovation. Her passion for helping leaders navigate the complexities of digital communication and hybrid workplaces makes her a sought-after expert in the field.

Together, David and Peggy offer a powerful blend of expertise in trusted leadership, communication, and practical, real-world application to enable leaders to thrive in today's evolving workplace.

Berrett-Koehler is an independent publisher dedicated to an ambitious mission: *Connecting people and ideas to create a world that works for all.*

Our publications span many formats, including print, digital, audio, and video. We also offer online resources, training, and gatherings. And we will continue expanding our products and services to advance our mission.

We believe that the solutions to the world's problems will come from all of us, working at all levels: in our society, in our organizations, and in our own lives. Our publications and resources offer pathways to creating a more just, equitable, and sustainable society. They help people make their organizations more humane, democratic, diverse, and effective (and we don't think there's any contradiction there). And they guide people in creating positive change in their own lives and aligning their personal practices with their aspirations for a better world.

And we strive to practice what we preach through what we call "The BK Way." At the core of this approach is *stewardship,* a deep sense of responsibility to administer the company for the benefit of all of our stakeholder groups, including authors, customers, employees, investors, service providers, sales partners, and the communities and environment around us. Everything we do is built around stewardship and our other core values of *quality, partnership, inclusion,* and *sustainability.*

We are grateful to our readers, authors, and other friends who are supporting our mission. We ask you to share with us examples of how BK publications and resources are making a difference in your lives, organizations, and communities at bkconnection.com/impact.

Dear reader,

Thank you for picking up this book and welcome to the worldwide BK community! You're joining a special group of people who have come together to create positive change in their lives, organizations, and communities.

What's BK all about?

Our mission is to connect people and ideas to create a world that works for all.

Why? Our communities, organizations, and lives get bogged down by old paradigms of self-interest, exclusion, hierarchy, and privilege. But we believe that can change. That's why we seek the leading experts on these challenges—and share their actionable ideas with you.

A welcome gift

To help you get started, we'd like to offer you a **free copy** of one of our bestselling ebooks:

bkconnection.com/welcome

When you claim your **free ebook**, you'll also be subscribed to our blog.

Our freshest insights

Access the best new tools and ideas for leaders at all levels on our blog at ideas.bkconnection.com.

Sincerely,

Your friends at Berrett-Koehler